Frances Darnell Whited

Footprints in the Dust
Stories from the Old Tuscaloosa Road

by
Frances Darnell Whited

Frances Darnell Whited

Copyright 2018
All rights reserved.
Frances Darnell Whited

Printed in the United States of America.
No part of this book may be used or reproduced in any manner whatsoever without written permission except in the case of brief quotations embodied in critical articles and reviews.

Fifth Estate
2795 County Hwy 57
Blountsville, AL 35031
First Edition
Cover Designed by An Quigley
Illustrations by Frances Darnell Whited
Printed on acid-free paper
Library of Congress Control No: 2018945500
ISBN: 9781936533541

First Edition 2018

Cover based on an Old Book, circa late 1800's.
The cover shows the author as she appeared as a child on the Tuscaloosa Road. The title page shows the Roberts girls on the Old Tuscaloosa Road.

Dedication

Whenever I see an old picture or drive down an old country road, my ancestors speak to me of stories and times gone by. I was very lucky I knew the families of both by mother and father, and my brother and I are part of their legacy. It is with a sense of gratitude I dedicate this book to the Roberts, Johnson, Green, and Grigsby families. In particular, it is dedicated to my mother, Martha Frances Johnson Grigsby and to my son, Bart Alston Rainey, who listened and smiled as I told these stories to him.

As will be evident at the end of these stories, it is the eulogy for my brother, Jerry Grigsby, whom I loved dearly.

Frances Darnell Whited

Acknowledgments

The manuscript of this book, **Footprints in the Dust**, was reviewed by many Blount County folks. Others heard me talk at length about it. Without their support, advice, warnings, and gentle guidance to improve the manuscript, it would never have become a real book.

We wish to thank the Blount County Historical Society for their support of this project.

Amy Rhudy, Curator at the Blount County Memorial Museum, came into my life when her son was in school. She became a major part of my journey to create a book about Old Tuscaloosa Road and the people of Blount County.

Rachel Ellis Dean, an honors graduate from Birmingham Southern College with a degree in English/Language Arts, edited this book. She was my "Grammar Police." She restored order to my rambling sentences, eliminated unnecessary words and phrases which interfered with the flow of reading and gave positive advice. I was delighted to learn her great-grandfather, Ercy Bellenger, lived on Tuscaloosa Road.

Beverly Ellis, a retired educator and assistant principal, knew what a challenge editing my manuscript would be and she helped anyway. Beverly surprised me with the knowledge she had lived on my Old Tuscaloosa Road. She was meant to be a part of this journey.

Leonard Yarbrough, a volunteer at the Blount County Memorial Museum, supported my writing and edited many photographs. His unique, sometimes challenging, questions helped provide clarity and focus while fitting everything together.

Laura Roberson, another volunteer at the museum, always had time to assist me with little details, and there were many! She also volunteered to read the manuscript. I appreciated her input. Laura spent afternoons with her parents learning to drive on sections of the Old Tuscaloosa Road.

Jerry Cornelius, also a museum volunteer, is a long-time friend and classmate. For two years, he listened to me talk about Old Tuscaloosa Road and traveled with me around Blount County in search of pictures and people. We joked and talked about the movie *"Driving Miss Daisy."*

When I planned a trip, I would phone him with the question, "Would you like to drive Miss Daisy today?"

My publisher, Joseph Lumpkin, with dry wit and gentle prods kept me focused on turning a collection of stories and snapshots into a book. To my amazement, I managed to blend family tales, historical events, and local miscellany into a coherent account of the life of a small girl, her gifted and troubled brother, and growing up in Blount County.

Jane Wright, a member of the Blountsville Historical Society, found me a treasure, a deed showing Old Tuscaloosa Road. The deed also showed Tuscaloosa Road to be separate from Huntsville Road.

Wilburn Beavers and Billy Fowler gave me more treasures: information, pictures, and deeds related to Tuscaloosa Road.

When I couldn't deal with modern technology, Barbara Williams, a kindly Wal-Mart employee, taught me how to get those pictures copied and out of my cell phone and tablet. She wanted no recognition, but, without her, there would be very few pictures.

Last, my family is where it all started. Martha Frances Johnson Grigsby, my mother, gave me strong roots. I did not realize how deep these roots were until I neared the completion of this book. My son, Bart Alston Rainey, listened to my doubts when I thought about chunking every page. Watching him grow up and learn the stories of our family has been an important part of my life – part of the legacy of family I gave him. I never fully understood how much I owe my family and its heritage until I saw the tapestry of life woven by the telling of these stories.

Thank you to Linda Thomas for the picture of Darnell and Martha used on the back cover.

Frances Darnell Whited

Preface

After supper in years gone by, folks settled in as the sun went down. For many families, there was a storyteller who provided entertainment when the day's work was over. Those storytellers might look around and say, "Come close, and I'll tell you a story." As a child, I heard stories told by family members. While they were not of historic importance or of great deeds, they created the setting for my life. The stories told were about kinfolks, neighbors, passers-by, and others were for entertainment.

When photography became available and more affordable to common people, they unknowingly began to document their lives with pictures. The picture boxes of Anna May Roberts Johnson and Martha Frances Johnson Grigsby are documentation of their ancestors and their ways of life. They span over a hundred years and help tell my family stories. As children, my brother and I sat on the floor and looked at these pictures.

The photographs in this book evoke memories of the dusty roads of my childhood. There are hundreds more waiting for a story. Each picture with its story gives insight to the people of our past. Maybe these stories will encourage others to search for their family pictures, packed away in dark closets across our county, and bring them out into the light to be shared, discussed, and enjoyed by future generations. Taken together, this is an account of coming of age, leaving home, facing change, and homecoming. Looking back, it almost is as if the dusty old road and I matured and grew older together. Certainly, the times and people defined who I have become. So, come close and listen as I tell of the voices echoing down the Old Tuscaloosa Road of Blount County, Alabama.

The Road Not Taken

By <u>Robert Frost</u> (1916)

Two roads diverged in a yellow wood,
And sorry I could not travel both
And be one traveler, long I stood
And looked down one as far as I could
To where it bent in the undergrowth;

Then took the other, as just as fair,
And having perhaps the better claim,
Because it was grassy and wanted wear;
Though as for that the passing there
Had worn them really about the same,

And both that morning equally lay
In leaves no step had trodden black.
Oh, I kept the first for another day!
Yet knowing how way leads on to way,
I doubted if I should ever come back.

I shall be telling this with a sigh
Somewhere ages and ages hence:
Two roads diverged in a wood, and I—
I took the one less traveled by,
And that has made all the difference.

This work is in the public domain of the United States because it was published before January 1, 1923.

Frances Darnell Whited

The Footprints (or Contents)

The Beginning

Dedication	3
Acknowledgements	4
Preface	6
Poem	7
The Footprints (or Contents)	8

Chapter 1 - Come Close and Listen — 11

The Way It Was	13
People and Places	15
Cleveland, Alabama	20
Indian Trails, Old Stagecoach Routes, and Dusty Roads	23
Looking both Ways on Old Tuscaloosa Road	26
Family Stories, Myths, and Outright Lies	30
Review of Alabama History	34

Chapter 2 - Footprints of the Roberts Family — 35

A Colorful Family	37
W. B. Roberts Estate and Transacting Business	42
Shade Trees of Old Tuscaloosa Road	45
Sugar, Coffee, and a Bit of Rationing	49
Droughts, Flash Floods, and Persistence	51
The Benefit of Not Having a Will	55
A Dapper Young Man - Another Arthur Roberts	60
Aunt Pearl Roberts	63
Uncle has a Moment	66
Finding Uncle Dewey	68
Aunt Etta Belle and Visiting Relatives	71
Aunt Eula Holt of Sugar Creek	74
Aunt Myrtle of Five Points	76
The Good Country Doctor	78

Chapter 3 - Footprints of the Johnson Family — 81

Albert and Anna (Roberts) Johnson Family	82
Bent nails	84
Hot Days and Johnson Ancestors	87
A pause for Joel Johnson	90

Love, Lice, Romance and those Johnson boys	93
Frances McGuire Johnson, a Strong Woman	96
A Revolutionary War Relative	99
Mad Dogs and Moss Bridge	102
Possum in a Pot	104
The Boat that Sailed Away	106
Uncle Ace: On Johnson Road	108
Ocean Sounds from the Past	111
Albert Johnson, the Gentle Trapper	113
Teacakes and Granny Anna's Kitchen	117
Anna's Post Card	121
Sassafras Tea, Rabbit Tobacco and Me	123
Blowgourd and 3 A.M in the Morning	125
Chocolate Covered Fried Ants	128
Minuteman Stamps	131
A White Horse Named Trigger	132
Chapter 4 - Footprints of the Green Family	**135**
The Greens from Hall County, Georgia	137
Another Green from Alvord, Texas	141
Out in Oklahoma	144
Who is Ona?	148
Waiting on Alvan and the Death of Grandma	150
Chapter 5 - Footprints of the Grigsby Family	**154**
Searching for the Grigsbys	155
So few Pictures	158
CCC Camps and the young Odell	160
Seasick and Overseas	162
The First Sunday in May	164
Hummingbirds	168
Aunt Fonnie's Story	171
A Handwritten History	173
A Trip Back in Time	175
Chapter 6 - My Footprints	**179**
A Girl Searching for Family	180
Barefoot Little Girl Toes and Chicken Business	182

Days in the Cotton Field	185
The Outhouse and the Old Milk Cow	188
Whispering Pines and Bee Stings in Clover	190
Smiling Musicians, Joe Rumore, and Radio	193
Terminals and Trains in Birmingham and Oneonta	195
Skunks around the Pot	198
Dish pans and the Drought	200
The Economics of Our Thanksgiving Turkey	203
My Mississippi Summer	206
Just a Critter	209
A Mystery in the Picture Box	212
Vittles, Fiddles and Bluegrass in the Front Yard	214
Oil mops, Radiators, and Cleveland School	217
Loafing and Cherry Vanilla Ice Cream	220
Postal Progress and Conversations with Edwina Pass Bryan	222
Talk of Tuscaloosa Road	225
Memories of Phenix City	227
Old County Church	230
Boyd's Music Shop and the Sounds of Life	232
Thundercloud and the Story I Could Not Write	235
Mental Health and Bryce Hospital	238
Another Piece of Tuscaloosa Road	241
Going for a Ramble	244
A Spanish Oak Tree and Two Southern Gentlemen	247
Old Dogs and an End to a Dusty Road	251
Epilogue	254
Appendix	256

Chapter One - Come Close and Listen

There are times when I get involved with trying to sort out who belongs to which family. I think everybody in Blount County is related to everybody else. Our shared family tree is much more like a blackberry thicket than it is a tree, and the briars can really get me all tangled up. I finally realized if I didn't arrange the setting of these stories "just right," I would end up with readers as confused and frustrated as I was at times while writing the stories.

So, we begin with the families I knew when I grew up and played with my brother in the dust of Old Tuscaloosa Road. I liken these families to a hutch of rabbits, for as an acquaintance once remarked to me, "Those of us engaging in genealogical rabbit hunting have learned we can only chase one rabbit at a time." On a good day, maybe, one might find one clue for a lost rabbit. As more is learned about the family, one's understanding of that family changes — sometimes (mostly) for the better and sometimes not so well. Different spellings of names crop up, driving the seeker to despair. For as many folks who are found and placed in the family tree, there will be twice as many who appear seemingly out of nowhere. Each of these needs to be documented, and the family list lengthens as time drags on. My family list continues to grow and change. Tomorrow, this list may be incorrect! For the moment, though, this is the hutch of rabbits for my stories.

The Way It Was

I soon learned I couldn't just sit down and start writing. I had to think about what I wanted to say, and many times, I simply had no clue where to start. Then, I had the idea of looking at those who had influenced me – the authors of the many books I had read, both for children and adults. They wrote so easily, or so it seemed as I re-read the lines they penned. After all, how hard could it be to write about Blount County, its people, my family, and a little bit of history?

Considering our lives, we are all a unique book of history. Our five senses give us stories of what we experience, but there is a problem with all this information, finding the right words to express what we have smelled, tasted, felt, heard, and seen. Where do we find perfect words to record our individual tales? This struggle for words can end the writing process. It's good to have someone around who thinks you can find those words, expressions, and vocabulary to convey what needs to be said. Many people helped each day. I am indebted to the people of Blount County and beyond who took time to talk with me.

Back in 2014, Robert Earl Woodard published his book, ***The Way It Was Back Then.*** I bought Earl's book because we worked together for many years. We joked, laughed, and sometimes talked about the way life was changing. I phoned Linda Head Shumate, my best friend, and a former guidance counselor. I told her about Earl's book. For years, she encouraged me to write down my stories, especially those about my brother, Jerry Grigsby. He was known around Blount County as Thundercloud.

An autographed copy of Earl's book went with me on my next trip to Linda's home in Belize in Central America. As friends of many years, we enjoyed sitting on the veranda of her Belizean home, talking for hours in the warm, Caribbean breeze. We watched the wild tropical trees and plants fill with birds I didn't know. We talked about growing up in the South and the changes we had seen. Linda was from Northport, and I was from Cleveland. Our lives were similar, but these areas of Alabama have their unique differences.

Both Earl Woodard and Linda Shumate got me thinking about those stories floating around in my Southern brain. I attended Earl's book signing in 2016 at Harold Dunn's Bloom-N-Pie event. As he signed another of his books for me, I told him about losing my best friend, Linda Shumate, to lung cancer.

After my goodbye, I enjoyed walking around the garden filled with daylilies in full bloom. I knew the Dunn family since childhood and had a great appreciation for their events. Country music played in the background, and the smell of homemade fried pies filled the air.

Darnell and Linda in Belize

I talked with Mr. Pate, who played music in my family's front yard on the Tuscaloosa Road. So many memories of the way it was back then came flooding back. Driving home, passing the Fowler Springs Church, then on past my homeplace on Tuscaloosa Road, I thought, "Where else in the world would there be a better place to find beautiful flowers, old friends from the past, real country music, and fried pies?" This was all here in Blount County, Alabama.

My Mom and Granny Anna taught me to save newspaper clippings. When I got home, I found the article I clipped from *The Blount Countian* advertising the June 15th event. I said a thank you to our local newspaper, Earl, and Linda. Together, they started me on the pathway from Tuscaloosa Road to the pages of my book.

A volunteer at the Blount County Memorial Museum knew how to ask difficult questions. Dr. Leonard Yarbrough challenged my weakening spirit with "thorny" questions! With his questions, he opened windows for me to see my writing with a clearer view.

I still struggle with these ideas, which are like delicate spider webs. Songs, books, newspapers, and people give me words. It becomes easier with helpful people in my life.

People and Places

The Old Tuscaloosa Road Today

As a little girl, I learned this old road, as my brother and I traveled with my family. When he learned to walk, we spent hours on the "Old Road," learning the language of our family, the unique dialect of our people, and ways of this area. I left the mountains of my home at age twenty and lived near the swamps and bayous in Louisiana. Then, I moved to the flat lands of Auburn. After several years, I returned to the beautiful mountains of my childhood to raise my son in the ways of Blount County. As I neared retirement, a plan for writing a book took shape. It was a vague idea without much direction and no structure. So, I wandered the unpaved roads of my ancestors, listening to the stories kinfolk and local folks told.

Most of my life was lived in the Cleveland community. I spent the greater part of my career immersed in children's literature, fascinated with the words of children's books. At some point, my mom gave me boxes and boxes of old family pictures, clippings, letters, and documents, many over a hundred years old, passed down from her mother, Anna Roberts Johnson.

Frances Darnell Whited

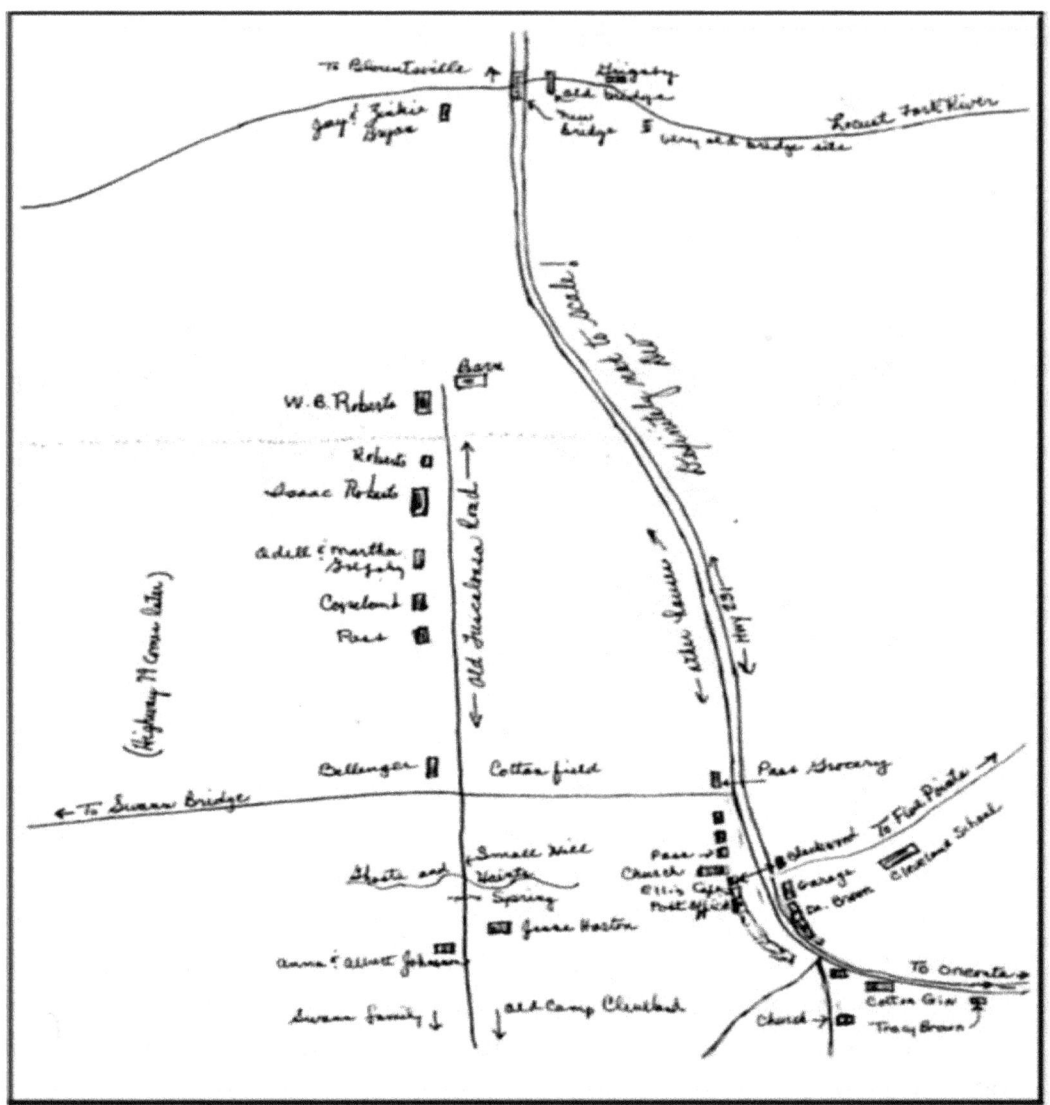

Darnell's Sketch of Cleveland, Alabama in the 1940's

As I pored over these artifacts of my family, I came to realize they had a story, a voice from the past. I began to travel down these old roads again with my ninety-four year old mother, visiting and talking with people of old Blount County. Relatives, who I never knew, became part of my daily life. Somehow, I would honor these people and their connections to the old roads of our area. Now, there's always one more picture, one more road with another story, waiting to be told. All I had to do was transcribe the stories of these pictures and records.

Many months of disappointment went by as I searched for the history of an old road, which would become the backdrop for my stories. It became the thin thread, which wove its way through my writing. "The Road" felt like a main character in a mystery. The search for an old map continued as there had to be one with this road's name on it. While sitting in a local cafe, looking at pages and pages of my typing, a friend asked the question, "Why do you give a hoot or a holler about that old road?" He was referring to the Old Tuscaloosa Road in Cleveland. The question stopped me, as we say in the South, "dead in my tracks." At the time, I didn't have a reasonable answer, not a clue, which only added to my own questions about the importance of having a dusty old road sauntering in and out of the pages of my plans for a book. It seemed to me this road must be important, or it would not occupy my thoughts and demand to have itself inserted into my family history. I started to wonder why I gave a 'hoot or holler' about the old road.

One rainy morning, while sipping my coffee, I very simply answered his question and mine. I recalled the days when, after supper, we gathered on the porch or in the living room, and one of the old folks – after we all settled down – began with, "Come close and listen to this story…," and then, continued on, riveting me as I sat on the floor. It was so obvious! The road wanted its story told, and its story is also my story. The road is not sentient, able to feel things, but I hear its voice and want that voice to be heard. It was a part of my family and my distant ancestors' daily lives.

It was once a trail, then an old stagecoach road that became the Old Tuscaloosa Road, renamed Tuscaloosa Pike. I eventually found its name on old family deeds. Many of our family pictures show "The Road" in the background. As a child, I roamed freely up and down it to visit my kinfolks who lived along "The Road." On dry Alabama days, its dust would rise up to bring me the unique smell only a dusty road can bring. That smell is still alive in my mind. If Daddy poured used car oil, or aircraft oil, in front of the house to minimize dust, we didn't have just the dusty smell, but we had the smell of old oil combined with dust. These smells waft in and out of my memories as if carried on a warm southern breeze. I cannot think of this old road without the scent of old oil mixed with the dust of the road coming to mind.

Without knowing it, I learned at a young age to listen for travelers on the road. They might stop and talk or tell some news they heard along the way. With my little brother by my side, we walked to neighbors and family homes. It was safe to visit as we pleased those people within walking distance. They were all looking out for two kids, but, we didn't know it. We could walk to Pass Grocery on Highway 231 with five cents for a special treat. We learned about storytelling and listening from the travelers and family who passed us. We saw the mail truck make its regular stops, sometimes filled with passengers in the covered truck bed. We heard the sounds dirt roads make, could taste and smell the dust, and feel the grit on our teeth. Dirt was part of traveling and seeing the dust rising in the distance was delightful. It meant someone was coming down the road. If you were fortunate, one day you would be honored to see a "dust devil," which looks like a baby tornado as it moves down a dirt road and disappears. Dust floated into each room of our home even with the doors and windows closed.

Many times, I looked at pieces of roadbeds in Blount County and wondered if that little bit could be another piece of my old road. Did it amble by Greens Chapel Cemetery where my Johnson and Green relatives were buried? It may have been there when Gilliland Store was built by Uncle Ace Johnson's daughter, Louise. As we go south of Cleveland, bits and pieces of an old roadbed are still visible, almost lost in the overgrown trees.

All roads lead somewhere, but The Old Tuscaloosa Road led to my family history. It taught me to love dusty roads. It showed me where I came from, guided me toward a future, and grounded me in a strong extended family. It was there as years passed and changes came to Cleveland, Blount County, and the Roberts, Johnson, Bryan, Pass, Green, Horton, Cornelius, Easley, and Grigsby families. Over the course of time, the characters who knew the road influenced my life, taught me to listen, and gave me a voice. A love for dusty old roads, family homeplaces, old pictures, and storytellers started on the Old Tuscaloosa Road. Echoes of children's voices from the past fill my imagination. We can't see them, but their absence stimulates our senses to learn more.

The quest to learn about this road and its people has taken over two years. Sometimes, it feels as if I knew each of them personally. Maybe, the reader will get better acquainted with them while we load our wagons and travel across the country with the Johnson, Green, Roberts and Grigsby families as they migrate to the State of Alabama.

Old dusty country roads are a vanishing thing. With pictures and stories, a voice can be given to these roads and the special dusty old road of my past, Old Tuscaloosa Road, and the people who knew it. With a few old pictures and words, we'll journey down less traveled roads and into the past of the place I called home. Do you know who you are, and where you came from? Did your long dead ancestors travel down the dusty roads of Blount County?

Long ago, I heard a song, and I listen to it often, "When the Music's Not Forgotten." The words inspire me each day as I write, "Please come close, for I long for you to hear the sound that will rid you of your fears." So now, please come close and listen with me for the sounds and voices that echo down the dusty roads of Blount County, Alabama. Let me introduce you to the people who knew these roads and the footprints they made.

Pass Grocery 2018

Cleveland, Alabama

Cover of Eldridge Bynum's Book

Whether we say we like "history" or not, it is what makes us who we are. I thought, in the beginning, my stories needed a bit of history. According to many historians, "Blount County was created by the Alabama Territorial legislature on 1818 February 6, from land ceded to the Federal government by the Creek Nation on 1814 August 9. It was named for Gov. Willie G. Blount of Tennessee, who provided assistance to settlers in Alabama during the Creek War of 1813-14." Many sources establish Alabama's statehood, "Alabama, which joined the union as the 22nd state in 1819…" In Eldridge Bynum's book, *Cleveland Alabama 35049*, he tells us what his research found about the history of my little hometown, Cleveland, Alabama. A copy of his book may be found at the Blount County Memorial Museum.

When the post office was organized in 1879, Cleveland was known as Anderton. Another name given to the area was Dry Creek Cross Roads. Nute Morris gave it the name around 1882 when he built a pine pole building, establishing the first business with dry goods. According to Bynum, a few years later John Blackwood bought the business and renamed the area Blackwood's Cross Roads. After a petition, a name change came again on January 9, 1890. The town of Cleveland was born, named for President Grover Cleveland.

Mother's copy of this book was stored in a box for several years. The pages have a yellow aged color and smell like old books usually do. The glue has become brittle, crumbles, and the pages fall out. I read it several times looking for the family names of Roberts, Green, Johnson, and Grigsby. To my disappointment, their names were not there, but there were pictures from my past.

You may ask if my book, with its stories and pictures, is a family history, the history of Cleveland, or a history of Blount County. I smile as I speculate maybe a bit of all, or maybe just rambling ideas placed on paper. With my background in education and library media, I have tried to be accurate. Are the stories one hundred percent accurate? I smile again. There may be some documentation, but the research used is only as accurate as the researcher and the documents from the past. Information may not be completely accurate when the oral history I love is included. Is oral history accurate? Well, this answer needs more than a smile. Sometimes it is, and sometimes it is embellished to make an interesting tale. It is a book of short stories and dusty trails which became old stagecoach roads. Some of the trails became modern highways.

(Photograph courtesy of the Blount County Memorial Museum)
Gene Blackwood's General Store ca 1940 - 50

The stories move us from horses to automobiles, from handwritten letters to computers, the coming of telephone lines, and on to television. It is about the changes in our homes and family life with memories of cold mornings around a wood stove. Old wooden outhouses disappear. Fresh water comes into our kitchens, and the family dipper is put away. Foods once stored in ice boxes find their ways into refrigerators. On a hot Alabama day, it's now cooler inside than under the favorite shade tree.

It is stories of when doctors made house calls, delivered babies at home, and followed the changes vaccinations gave the world. We follow other changes. Now, death from the flu seldom occurs. States passed compulsory attendance laws for school enrollment and vaccinations. 'Mad dogs' wandering down roads would be no more. Our pets are now vaccinated for rabies, and we don't worry about mad dogs anymore.

Our families' history, whether completely accurate or not, is part of the history of our world, and it changes with our personal interpretations. It may be confusing, and sometimes unclear, who these kinfolk and acquaintances from the past really were.

Indian Trails, Old Stagecoach Routes, and Dusty Roads

My childhood revolved around the old dirt road going past our place. I grew up on what is now called Tuscaloosa Pike in Cleveland, Alabama. All my life, I could see the remains of this old road that went past the Roberts family property, my parents' house, and on past my grandparents' home. Was it visible at Jay and Zinkie Bryan's house near the river bridge on Highway 231 going to Blountsville? It was near the old Grigsby homeplace on the right above the bridge. There were bits and pieces of a road going south of Cleveland and below Green's Chapel Church and Gilliland's Store. I was interested in the remains of this road all my life.

In a conversation with Stanley Moss, the president of the Blount County Historical Society, I mentioned my interest in the old roads of Blount County. He told me about Mary Gordon Duffee's book, *Sketches of Alabama*. My career in education had been focused on children's literature, and I missed reading this book. Frankly, I had never heard of it. One day, after several visits to the Blount County Memorial Museum, working on other projects, I asked Amy Rhudy, the museum curator, about the book. She found it in the Museum's collection of books, and I sat down with Duffee's stories of her past. I lost myself reading about her. She wrote about the Tuscaloosa Road, as she journeyed from Tuscaloosa to Blount Springs in the eighteen hundreds. Could the pieces of my old road be part of the Tuscaloosa Road in her book? This opened more avenues of thought for

Cover of Mary Gordon Duffee's Book

Frances Darnell Whited

me, and I had to have my own personal copy. After searching the internet, I was able to obtain my copy. When my book arrived in the mail, it had been in the San Fernando Valley State College Library, and the last time it was checked out was 1979. It had now come home to Alabama!

With my copy of this historical book, I was free to spend time with its pages, reading and rereading certain words, phrases, and paragraphs, in search of Tuscaloosa Road. Duffee states on pages 19-20 when she refers to Jonesboro pioneers and her travels to Blount Springs, "On the other side of the Tuscaloosa Road, which formed the main avenue of Jonesboro, lived Samuel A. Tarrant, a native of South Carolina." She wrote about leaving Jonesboro through a long land, which became very rocky. Her route continued on to the old village of Carrollsville, and she compared it to the early days of a trading center like Bucksville. With her words, I became part of Duffee's journey to Blount Springs, rumbling along toward Carrollsville. Duffee explains on page 24, "Mrs. Nabers, widow of Francis Drayton Nabers, had lived in her present home on the Tuscaloosa Road at Carrollsville since her marriage in 1825."

Before this book, my interest was focused on family ancestors. I had inherited my mother's and her mother's numerous boxes of old pictures. There was something magical about holding these aging photos. They could be spread out across my dining room table and touched. The smell of old papers would float up. There was seldom a name associated with a picture. The old black albums were turning to dust. These women from my past were also keepers of old papers and letters. There was no organization. It was a paper soup of stuff in boxes! At first, hours and hours of identifying these long dead characters was fun. One day, I realized, it had become a gigantic chore. I asked myself, "Why am I doing this, and will anyone after me care who these old people were?" These people and the old road were important to me. Days passed, and again, I questioned if I were going to be the last one to care. Sometimes, after hours of frustration and sorting, it would all be boxed up again and put out of sight for days, even weeks.

The old road would not give me peace, and it wanted to be the center of the stories I began to write about my family, Cleveland, and Blount County. I planned a trip to Wallace State to start researching old stagecoach roads that ran across Blount County, but my brother got very sick again. The old road left me in peace during his sickness and death. I pulled the boxes out, looking for pictures of my brother to use at his funeral. There, in a box, was an old deed Mom kept. It described the boundaries for the place where my Granddaddy Johnson's house was located on the Old Tuscaloosa Road!

On the Road

Looking Both Ways on Old Tuscaloosa Road

Mother had a picture of me standing in the dust of old Tuscaloosa Road. In the background was a barn. There's a bow in my short brown hair. I'm wearing a dress Mom made for me. She said I was a serious child, never causing any trouble but curious with lots of questions. We had many kinfolks with stories. I liked talking with older people and stood around waiting for them to talk to me.

Darnell, Looking Right

As I stood in front of the Roberts's homeplace in the picture, looking to the left or right down the long road, it was easy to see it led to my family. Behind me was the Isaac Roberts's home with its out buildings. Born in 1866, he was my great-grandfather. Isaac's brother, Arthur Roberts, had a house to my left. If I looked across the field, the Cleo Pass family home was there. Cleo's mother, Lula Jane, was Isaac's sister. I could turn to my right and know the home of my grandpa, Albert Johnson, would be way down the unpaved dusty road.

My brother and I learned to walk this road at a young age. We rode bicycles up and down it. There was so much dust in hot Alabama summers. It left our legs with a dusty orange glow. There was always mud after a rain and lots of puddles. Large rocks washed up out of the chert and make bicycle riding hazardous. Both my brother and I have the scars to prove it. Our knees were often bloody from a fall while walking, running, or riding on the road.

For those who do not know about "chert," it is mined across the state of Alabama and used as a cheap way to cover a road. A fine-grained sedimentary rock, it has an old history covering roads in Alabama. Depending on where it came from, it could contain fossils and crystals of quartz. My brother and I collected the fossils and shiny quartz then stored them in shoe boxes under our beds.

Mom gave advice for preventing bloody knees from falls. "Don't run! Just slow down!" As kids, we had trouble with that advice. My parents didn't worry about where we played, bicycled, or visited along the road. The old road in Cleveland, Alabama, was a safe place to grow up. When we left the house each day, Mom would simply say, "Take care of your little brother." And, we were off for an adventure. My childhood memories revolve around this road. The road seems to want its story told to others about the families we knew and with whom we grew up.

After my great-great-grandfather, William Bazzle Roberts's survival of the Civil War, he and his wife, Martha Jane, left Georgia for Alabama. Their wagon train brought them to Blount County where they raised their family of nine children on the road. I found the children's names in **The Heritage of Blount County, Alabama, Vol. 5.** In my imagination, I see Arthur, Dora, Lula Jane, Isaac, James J., C. L., Joady, Sarah, and Julia as they walk down the same road I walked. They laughed and played in the same fields my brother and I played in so many years later.

Isaac Roberts, and his wife, Martha Liberty Green, built their home nearby and raised their family there. Their children: Dewey, T. C., Pearl, Myrtle, Lula, Etta Belle, and Anna would be part of huge family gatherings at the Roberts's house on the road. Anna, my grandmother, played in the fields and rambled the old road. Except for Pearl, all of Isaac's children left the old house. Pearl stayed until the house was falling in and only left when she had a stroke.

Dewey Roberts's daughter, Eula Jean Copeland, gave me a copy of a picture believed to be taken in front of Isaac's house. On my visit to Jean's home near Blountsville, Mother and Jean spent time talking about their memories of the Roberts's family and Dewey's children. They decided the picture of a horse and buggy was definitely in front of Isaac's house. I learned about Jean's sisters and their interest in the

Roberts and Green ancestors. She gifted me with flowers from her yard, and I left her home with new pictures and more ideas.

At Jean's driveway, instead of going back to Blountsville, I took a right turn and drove slowly down the county road toward Garden City, looking for the house from my memories of Uncle Dewey. It was still there, so I stopped in a nearby driveway. As I turned around to head home, I looked up at the road sign naming the dusty road in front of me, "Guinn's Cove Road." Mother couldn't understand my excitement. With her hearing loss, it can sometimes be hard to get my words across. Last year, we took a ramble down to Nectar. A "ramble" is usually a walk for pleasure, especially in the countryside. The word has been around since the sixteen hundreds. Now, we can ramble in vehicles, down a course with many turns. That day we made a few right hand turns to find the cemetery where Joel Johnson was buried. We found this graveled dirt road on that trip, but we were looking for Johnson ancestors at the time. Being two little old gray-haired ladies on the back roads of Blount County, we decided it was best to stay with the paved roads. We didn't venture down the dusty path. Whether it was fate, luck, or divine intervention, something bought me back to the other end of Guinn's Cove Road. Well, again, where the pavement ends, another road begins. It was another old road from the past of my ancestor, Joel Johnson, born around 1795. My search for the people of Tuscaloosa Road led me to yet another old dusty family road that influenced both the Roberts and Johnson families.

In my mind, I'm back again on Tuscaloosa Road, in Cleveland, with my little brother by my side. We are walking to Grandpa Albert Johnson's house, a city block away and down a very small hill. The road is covered over with trees, low hanging limbs and a wet weather spring. Jesse Horton's house is on the left before we get to Grandpa's. Mr. Horton is a distant relative. Many nights, Grandpa told us ghost stories about the shady area at the foot of the hill near the Horton's house. Most of the time, we walked pretty quickly when we passed Mr. Jesse's place. We don't slow down because of Grandpa's vivid stories about the hollow at the foot of the hill being haunted. It has a 'haint' the old folks declared live there. And, you may ask, what is a 'haint'? It is pure Southern colloquialism; the word 'haint' means a ghost, an apparition, or lost soul.

The hollow is always cooler and darker with those low overhanging trees. This just added to the idea of a 'haint' being there. Around Halloween, the falling leaves crunch under our feet, at times touching our arms or legs before hitting the ground. This caused us to run past Mr. Jesse's house with the mystery of the haunted hollow alive in our young minds.

I remember Grandpa told us stories of prisoners from Old Camp Cleveland that used to be below his house. The camp was built around 1935 in a field owned by Mr. Blackwood, and it housed black prisoners. I don't remember the buildings. They were probably already gone. I do remember Grandpa said he felt sad for the prisoners because they were away from their families. There is now a street named "Camp Road" near the old site.

When I was a child, sassafras grew in abundance on the banks of the road. Granny Johnson used the roots to make tea. Today, the road is paved and houses replace the old fields. There is even a grocery store near the site of the prison. The 'haints' have probably moved to a more isolated place to haunt. Albert Johnson's house, remodeled with running water and indoor plumbing, remains up the road from the site of the old camp. At the other end of the road, nothing remains of Isaac's house. Arthur's house and barn are still standing, now remodeled by new owners. I smile and think maybe the 'haints' of long ago are finally at peace under the trees around Uncle Arthur's shady place at the end of Old Tuscaloosa Road.

Family Stories, Myths, and Outright Lies

It is time to introduce three folks who are main characters from the Tuscaloosa Road: Albert Johnson, Odell Grigsby, and Martha Grigsby. A family of storytellers greatly influenced my childhood, but these three were the most outstanding.

Growing up in Cleveland in the 1940's and 50's gave me a love and respect for storytelling. Nights were long and quiet. There was no television for us until the late 50's. I remember when a neighbor got the first one I had ever seen. My brother and I could see the flicker of light from the house windows when the

Albert & Anna (Roberts) Johnson

sun went down. My great-aunt, Pearl Roberts, and I sat on the porch at the old Roberts's homeplace and talked about this magic box she heard about on radio. It had sound and showed pictures in your living room. Without television, we talked to each other a lot. Family members passed on stories they heard. Sometimes, they invented a few, and we listened. Listening for a story developed a form of patience and fired our young imaginations. When family members sat down and started to talk, we just waited and hoped for a new tale. Even the ones we heard before were often new again with the significance of being repeated. It didn't really matter if the story was the total truth, especially if it came from our silver-haired grandpa.

The best storyteller, in my opinion, was my grandpa, Albert Johnson. He was born in 1885. Spending the night with Grandpa and Granny meant hearing stories from Grandpa. His stories could've been Grimm's Fairy Tales for the effect they had on my brother and me. These tales guaranteed we didn't roam far from home. Granny said her goodnight, and said, "Now, Albert, don't scare the children." Then, she would go to sleep. He enjoyed sitting in his chair, with a dip of snuff, and entertaining his two grandchildren with a tale. We expected him to have a story for us. He was the authority on family tales. It would be many years later, after we grew up, when we began to know the difference between fact and fiction. Even then, it didn't matter if it were words from our blue-eyed grandpa. Grandpa's house had double fireplaces, back to back, one in the living area and one in a bedroom. We never slept in a room with a fireplace. We were sure something would come down the chimney and drag us up and carry us off. Before we went to sleep, we said our prayers on our knees. We prayed a black panther wouldn't crawl down and find us. It was nice to see the sun come up at Grandpa's house.

My dad, Odell Grigsby, was born in 1919 and grew up in the Blountsville area near the bridge over the Locust Fork River. He was the second best storyteller in my life. His stories were about hard times in his life and days around the river. His house burned when he was a little fellow.

They lost everything to the fire, and the family was divided up and lived with neighbors in the community. Dad was always afraid of fire but became a fireman at Hayes International, in Birmingham, working there for thirty-six years. An article in *The Blount Countian* gave him credit for starting the first fire department in Cleveland. Fire was always his enemy, and he told us stories of fires at the Birmingham Airport. He told us about being seasick on a ship carrying him to the Panama Canal during World War II. My dad's favorite story to tell us was about a Native American great-grandmother from Georgia. He searched most of his adult life for records to prove this story he heard as a child. He passed this tale on to me with all his research. The search is still on-going to prove this story and find that Native American ancestor.

Born in 1923, my mother, Martha Frances Johnson Grigsby, at the time of this writing is ninety-four years old. She is a great storyteller.

Martha (Johnson) Grigsby

Her family's colorful history has been passed down from other ancestors like Joel Johnson, born in 1795; Thomas Benton Green, born in 1837; and William Bazzel Roberts, born in 1846. Their stories are documented in books about history of Blount County. Many of the stories in this book were told to me by my mother. My Grandpa and Daddy lived again as these stories were told and re-told to me, sometimes with added information and embellished with her sense of humor. Road trips with Mom evoked memories as we drove along old county roads looking for cemeteries, bridges, roads, and old homeplaces.

It may be trite to say this, but my brother and I always felt richer after hearing family stories. This is how our family shared a part of themselves with us. They gave us a love for stories and storytelling. Sometimes, I drop into a story, look around, and notice folks aren't interested. I have learned they don't have a family full of storytellers and old tales. They don't seem to appreciate and respect the give and take of a good story, and I feel sad for those people. They had no 'Mad Dogs' wandering about, no black panthers (sometimes called painters) to drag them off, or 'haints' roaming their roads and filling their memories. They had no hungry Confederate soldiers making their way home, no unfound Native American ancestors. For me, life would be sad without the tradition of storytelling.

When building my home for retirement, I wanted a porch, a place to sit and think of stories, maybe share a tale with my son. I have the porch with a ceiling painted a color named "Haint Blue." There is a bottle tree with blue bottles and other blue items hanging around my property. You may wonder why blue: It's symbolic of water. Of course, I'm not superstitious, but everybody knows a 'haint' can't cross water. I live peacefully with these imaginary 'haints' and my family's stories as I scribble old tales from my memories. I sip a morning coffee with my son on the front porch. So far, no 'haints' have bothered us!

Roberts Family
Eula, Myrtle, Pearl
Isaac, Dewey, Arthur, Etta Belle, Anna, Martha, T. C.

Review of Alabama History

Before we go any further, we need a brief review of Alabama History. A search of Wikipedia states, "Alabama has had five political capitals during its history. The first was the territorial capital in St. Stephens in 1817, followed by the state convention in Huntsville in 1819, then the first "permanent" capital in Cahaba in 1820. It was then moved to Tuscaloosa in 1826, until coming to rest in Montgomery in 1846."

Traveling on the Old Tuscaloosa Road

Chapter Two - Footprints of the Roberts Family

Some old roads of Alabama cannot be documented with their name on a map. The history of Alabama and Blount County is combined with the history of these roads. To get to Blount County, our ancestors may have traveled on the Bear Meat Cabin Road, the Tennessee Road, the Georgia Road, the Huntsville Road, or the Federal Road. Pieces of these old trails and roads can still be seen, disappearing along our paved highways. My interest focused only on the Tuscaloosa Road, its pieces in Blount County, and its connection to my ancestors and me.

Long, long ago, the James Roberts family left the state of Virginia, and moved to North Carolina. A few years later, a family story records James Roberts and his wife, Sarah Wisdom Roberts, left North Carolina with their children in a two wheeled cart, following worn trails to Georgia where they established their family. The Civil War came to Georgia. The grandson of James, William, enlisted during the War. After the war, William with his family left the recovering state of Georgia in a wagon train, heading to Blount County around 1870. They settled on what was to be called the Old Tuscaloosa Road.

Frances Darnell Whited

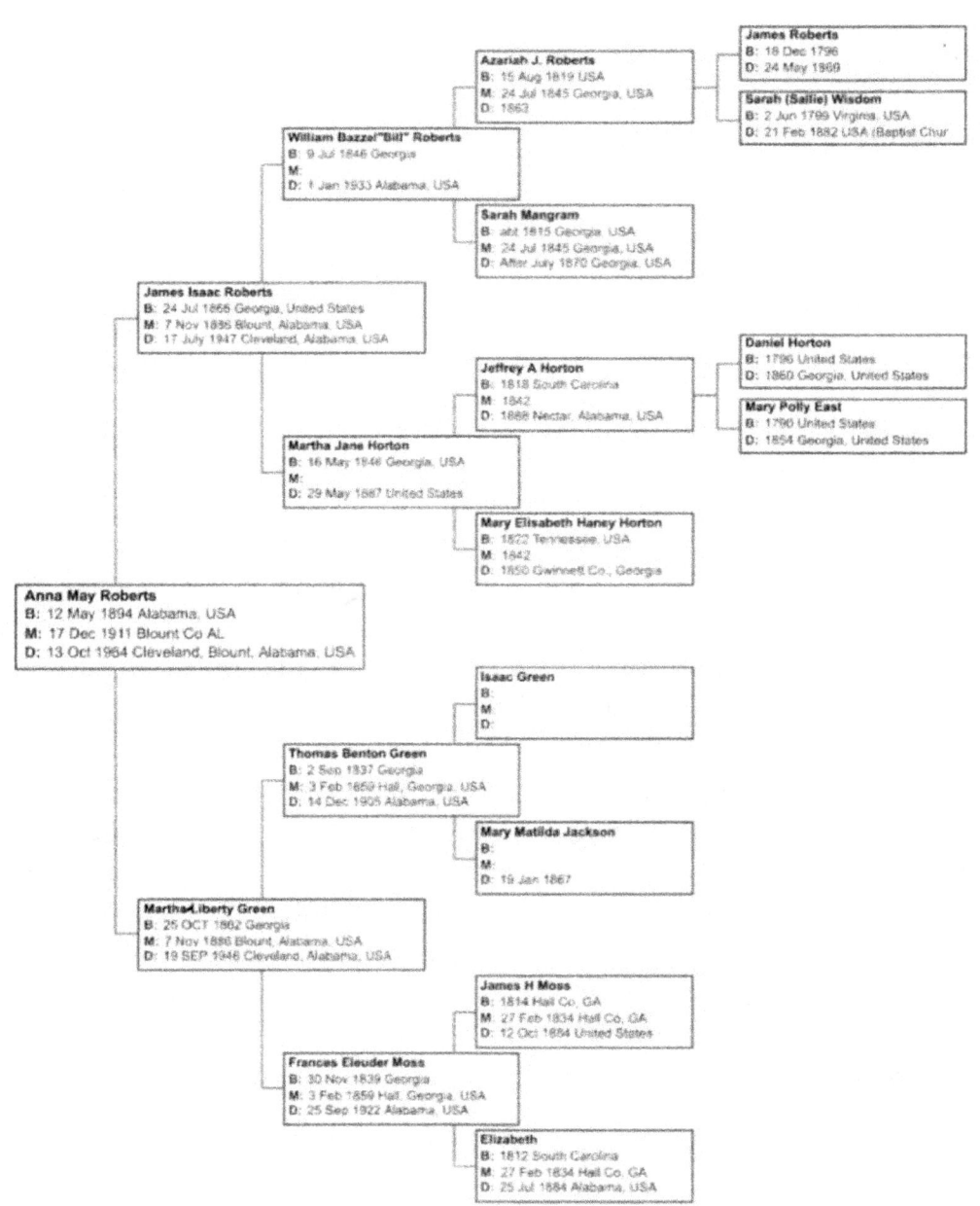

A Colorful Family

Someone once said in reference to my family they were "colorful." It was a whisper, said in a low voice, not meant for my ears. At the time of the low murmuring, I listened. I don't think the individual meant vivid, lively, dramatic, or animated. It seemed to mean "controversial," possibly notorious. I felt a bit offended at the use of the word "colorful." Some time was needed to think about the way the conversation offended me. After that bit of pondering, I decided I liked "colorful family." With documentation pieced together from many sources, I found my "colorful" family fought in wars for their homeland, migrated across the undeveloped country in wagons, produced many successful and interesting ancestors, valued family life, and founded churches. There were a few who strayed and wandered off the law-abiding path, but most were peaceful, respectable farming folks. That day the offending individual's words became just that, words…words for a story about my "colorful" family. "Colorful" began to make me smile, and I looked for it in pictures of the kin who knew Tuscaloosa Road.

One "colorful" example of my family is the from Roberts family. Early records of Azariah Roberts state he was born August 15, 1819, and he died around 1863. His father was probably named James

James Isaac and Martha Liberty Roberts

Roberts (December 18, 1796 - May 24, 1869). We know James married Sarah "Sallie" Wisdom. Thanks to research conducted by the Pass family and other family members, a wonderful story about James is recorded *The Heritage of Blount County, Alabama, Vol 5*. Sallie was the daughter of a wealthy, Virginia planter and had a dowry of four slaves. In 1818, at the time of their marriage, James would not accept the slaves and moved with his new wife to North Carolina. James moved his family one more time to Gwinnett County, Georgia, "where the grass hits the horse's belly." Did his courage to refuse to be part of slavery change his future?

We found plenty of information about Azariah's son, William Bazzel "Bill" Roberts, born in Georgia on July 9, 1846, with oodles of documentation about his life as a Confederate soldier. The picture used in most books shows Bill in his Masonic apron, with the fold pointed down. Masses of gathered facts were written about the Masons, sometimes reflecting good, and at other times, controversial. While reading about the history of this organization, I found George Washington was a member of a Virginia Lodge. And, could we imply that good ole' George was a "colorful" character?

My favorite story about Bill is recorded in the pages of *Miscellaneous Confederate Soldiers from in and Around Blount County*. He stated in an interview, "I got home on the 28th of April. I made a little crop." He had seen battles at Chickamauga, Knoxville, Lynchburg, and Richmond. He stated he was never in the hospital. He was one of the lucky soldiers of the war, for many died not in battle but from disease. Recently, I read the most common foe was "the mumps, measles, and other forms of illness."

Bill survived the war, was with Lee at the surrender at the Appomattox Court House, and came home to Georgia to make a little crop! Dangers would have been many, scenes of blackened ruins filled his travels, smells of war would have overwhelmed his senses, and he most likely walked from the Appomattox Court House to his home in Georgia. His courage and stamina made him a very "colorful" character. I read somewhere soldiers pinned their names on their clothes to avoid being buried in an anonymous grave. Did this returning man pin his name on his clothes? My imagination creates images of him in his worn, dusty clothes making his way home. He most likely heard about Sherman's March across Georgia, and perhaps, wondered if his family was there. I visualize his family waiting and hoping for his return. And, he made a little crop!

I've asked myself why he moved to Alabama. We believe he heard about Alabama from friends and relatives. As the head of his household, did he wake up one morning with the idea, and moving became a certainty? That afternoon, as the sun set with a golden glow in the west, he may have decided it was time to leave Georgia. Probably, that year's crops were finished. He packed up his family and a few necessary household goods and began the journey from Georgia. Did his family travel in a wagon train with others looking for a better life? When they came as settlers tumbling along, were they looking for good farming spots? These were the foothills of the Appalachian Mountains, taken from Native Americans. Did they know the horrors of the "Trail of Tears" and cruelty forced on the true owners?

The wide valleys and coves held their dreams. I have tried to picture uprooting his family and traveling for days and days down dusty trails to reach Blount County, Alabama. When they got to the spot of their dreams, how did they live until a home was built? In my mind's eye, I see a fireplace in later years on a cold winter's night and echoes from the journey filling their thoughts, and maybe telling listeners warming by the fire. It's only right I should wish to be sitting around the fireplace to hear these stories as they were told back then.

William Bazzel Roberts
(Article retyped with permission of the Blount County Historical Society, Oneonta, AL)

William Bazzel Roberts, with his Masonic Apron

"William Bazzel Roberts, an early Blount pioneer was born 9 July 1846 in Gwinnett County, Georgia. He was the son of Azariah (Ezariah) J. Roberts b. 15 Aug 1819 in NC and (m. 24 July 1845) and married Sarah Mangram. He was the grandson of James Roberts (18 Dec 1796 - 24 May 1869) and Sarah "Sallie" Wisdom (2 June 1799 – 21 Feb 1882). James and Sallie Roberts had come about 1822 from North Carolina to Gwinnett County. James owned and farmed land just north of Suwannee. Family folklore has it that Sallie was a daughter of a wealthy Virginia planter and her dowry for her 1818 marriage to James was to be four slaves, but James who objected slavery, would not accept them and moved his bride to North Carolina. A few years later, James, Sallie and two small children left North Carolina in a two-wheel cart to stop "where the grass hits the horse's belly", thus Gwinnett. James and Sallie are buried in the Old Suwannee Baptist Church Cemetery.

Azariah and his first born, William B. Roberts would enlist during the Civil War. Azariah would not return to his family, losing his life fighting for the confederacy. William B. Roberts who enlisted as a young teen at Stone Mountain, GA, would later surrender under General Robert E. Lee at Appomattox, VA.

After the war, William returned to Gwinnett and married Martha Jane Horton, 16 May 1846 - 29 May 1887, daughter of Jeffrey and Elizabeth Haney Horton. William B. and Martha Jane along with a small wagon party would migrate to Blount County around 1870. It is believed Martha Jane's family had migrated to Blount County earlier from Gwinnett and she wished to move to the area after her marriage. Family stories handed down suggest it did not please the Roberts family for William to move away. But it was in the Cleveland area William and Martha Jane would raise their family. Their children were James J., Julia, Sarah, Dora, Joseph, C.L., Isaac R., Lula Jane m. James Marshall Pass, and William Arthur. Martha Jane died few months after Arthur's birth. Later that year William B. married Mary Jane Cornelius who would raise the small children.

William B. Roberts was known affectionately in the county as "Uncle Bill". Longtime resident Mrs. Thelma Blair remembers a family in Cleveland that had a fever. No one wanted to go near them for fear of catching the deadly disease. "Uncle Bill" would go and take care of the young children and coming home would change clothes at the edge of the field to protect his own family. Bill Roberts would later help bury that family on Flat Top Mountain. He took an active part in county politics and considered it a privilege to do so. He served many years on the Blount County Board of Registrars. He was one of the sixteen charter members of Cleveland First Baptist Church. He was also a member of the Dry Creek Masonic Lodge, standing high in that order.

Descendants of Bill and Martha Jane Roberts still reside in the Cleveland area…William B. "Bill" Roberts passed away on January 1, 1933. He is remembered for his love of community, church, home and his God. This he showed in the unselfish way he lived. *Submitted by; Book Committee and Written by Charles A. Pass"*

Frances Darnell Whited

W. B. Roberts Estate and Transacting Business

Years and years ago, Mom gave me Isaac Roberts's family Bible. This book was a family treasure. It belonged to her beloved grandfather. It had been passed down to her from her mother, Anna. As a child, I remember carefully turning the pictures of this beautifully illustrated book. The illustrations were so alive; a person didn't have to read to know the stories from the "Good Book." These amazing drawings told the events of Biblical times. The pages were already becoming brittle when I sat on the floor as young girl, gently turning each page for my little brother and me. It had a place for birthdays, marriages, and deaths, so we knew about our folks from opening to that spot in the book.

When Mom passed it on to me, I had no idea what to do with it or how to preserve it. It stayed in a heavy clear, plastic bag, zipped up, in a drawer for years. One morning, I made a major decision to get all the pictures from my life out of the drawers in my house. Organization was going to come to my pictures. Names put on the backs and filed by subject or family. I wouldn't leave boxes of photos of strangers for my son to try to identify. While working my way in and out of forgotten storage places, I saw the old Bible just as I had left it, safely in the drawer. I tenderly lifted it out and took pictures of the pages of family history. I placed it back in the bag when I noticed a slight bulge, a few pages turned down maybe? There, in the slight bulge, were papers from 1940 and some dated even earlier. One folded paper caught my attention. A new story was found.

W. B. Roberts (Bill) died January 1, 1933, according to my research. The folded and scribbled on paper was a letter from an attorney dated January 11,

W. A. Roberts Barn on the Old Tuscaloosa Road

1940, seven years after his death. Was the estate of Bill now in dispute? That would make for a noteworthy family tale. As he entered his later years, Bill deeded his property to his son, Arthur. Yes, he left all of his worldly goods to his youngest child, leaving all his other children out of any inheritance. Arthur came home from Auburn University to take care of the stepmother who reared him, and he continued to live with his father after her death. He cared for his aging father until his passing. We read the attorney's plan…"establishing the mental incapacity of Mr. W. B. Roberts." I've been told the family had a disagreement after Arthur's return from college to care for his stepmother. It may be this led to the letter being written, or the fact, Arthur inherited everything.

Whatever the matter, this story would not let me rest. Sometimes, when I was working on a story, on a good day, I found a clue, other times I would just wish for one – any clue would do! Finally, a day came for a trip to Wal-Mart to get more pictures processed. There, pushing a cart down a far aisle was Joan Pass Ellis. Joan is descended from Lula Jane Roberts Pass, a daughter of Bill. We shared the same "Bill." Lula had a son named Cleo Pass. Cleo married and had a son named Amos. Amos married and had twin girls, Joan and Jane. What an extremely complex family tree our ancestors created! Joan's account of the letter of 1940 was simple, "I remember Granddaddy Pass talking about the house and land. As I remember, he and John may have testified about Bill Roberts intentions in wanting Arthur to have it." There is more to learn about W. B. Roberts and his youngest child, Arthur Roberts, the Auburn student who had to leave college without getting his degree.

William Arthur Roberts
(Article retyped with permission of the Blount County Historical Society, Oneonta, AL)

"William Arthur Roberts was the son of William "Bill" Bazzel Roberts and Martha Jane Horton. They came to Blount County, Alabama from Gwinnett County, Georgia in a wagon train in 1869. He was the grandson of Azariah (Ezariah) Roberts who died in the Civil War and son of James Roberts who was born in North Carolina and died in Gwinnett County, Georgia. William Arthur was born September 6, 1886.

William Arthur Roberts was raised in Cleveland, Alabama, by his father's second wife, Mary Jane Cornelius, after his mother died when he was 6 months old.

He was inducted into the U.S. Army on December 7, 1917 and served at the age of 31 years old in Company M 346 Infantry and Company D 59th Infantry. He was severely injured in battle while serving overseas on July 19, 1918. He was discharged with a disability on December 17, 1918. Because the heels of his feet were severely injured, the rest of his life was spent walking on the balls of his feet. He appeared to walk with a hop. He received the Purple Heart for his service in World War I.

He attended Auburn University on a disability grant from the government and spent over three years pursuing a degree in agriculture. He left with only a few months left until he received his degree. Auburn University records say he left to transfer to another school but he never returned to complete his degree. He came back home to Cleveland and led a rather reclusive life on the family farm.

Arthur Roberts died of a massive heart attack on December 23, 1961 on the way back from his daily walk to the Post Office in downtown Cleveland. He was a member of Cleveland First Baptist Church and is buried in Cleveland Methodist cemetery next to his mother and father. *Submitted by: Charles A. Pass*"

Shade Trees of Old Tuscaloosa Road

There is one story which certainly must be told about the people who knew the shade trees of the Old Tuscaloosa Road: the story of the Roberts family. To know them, we have to know their history and untangle a web of information. The Roberts folks were many. They had huge family gatherings under the old shade trees at the James Isaac Roberts home. We might say these are "witness trees," for the old trees witnessed the history of a family on Tuscaloosa Road. Their gatherings under the shade trees were another opportunity to listen and hear the voices of my family as they told each other the family news, expressed strong emotions about the world events and politics, and shared food the ladies prepared. Babies cried, children played, and folks lounged on old quilts spread under the trees.

James Isaac, son of William Bazzel "Bill" Roberts, married Martha Liberty Green. They farmed and raised their family down the road from Bill. Their children were: Dewey, Arthur, Pearl, Eula, Myrtle, Etta Belle, Anna May, and T. C., who we called Tessie. When the family of James Isaac got together at the old homeplace, the yard was full of people and laughter. My Granny Anna's picture box holds photographs of them. There were lots of other pictures of unidentified young men. I asked my mom who all these folks were. "Well, you know all the girls had boyfriends. Then, they got married except Pearl." And, as an afterthought, she asked, "Did I tell you Grandma Roberts could blow out fire? And she could stop a nose bleed or a bleeding when you pulled a tooth." At this point, I lost my train of thought, gone off on another tangent, and digressed to another topic! What I could reply was only, "No, Mom, I didn't know that." And, she talked on about Grandma Roberts's abilities, and I forgot about the shade tree story.

Superstitions and legends fill my family's past, and these stories could overflow into another book. Pausing in my writing, I did a little research on the old time art of healing and the tales surrounding this art. Amazement filled my reading, for I discovered this art is still alive and a strong tradition in some areas of our country. Blowing out fire, whooping cough, and warts was a well known practice in Grandma

Roberts's day. My mother keeps the Bible verse, Ezekiel 16:6-9, on a slip of paper. The verse includes the followings words, "(6) *And when I passed by thee, and saw thee polluted in thine own blood, I said unto thee when thou wast in thou blood, Live; yea, I said unto thee when thou wast in thy blood live… (9)"Then washed I thee with water; yea, I thoroughly washed away thy blood from thee, and I anointed thee with oil.*" She told me if anyone ever had a nose bleed or a bleeding from pulling a tooth, reading these words would stop the bleeding. Her grandma told her that.

Growing up, I knew about the healing power of tobacco juice. Was this handed down to me? To cure insect stings, the healer who chews or dips tobacco spits tobacco juice on the angry spot. Was my Grandma Roberts considered a healer? As the memories came flooding back, I remembered my brother was carried to a lady who lived beyond Swann Bridge because she could rid him of warts.

Mother uses the phrase, "Something just told me…,"and sometimes she would know "something." It would happen. She passed this on me, and at times, we have shared "something just told me" moment. I started calling this "a small quiet voice." There was no scientific, logical explanation for the "knowing." Without making any connection to the past, I taught my son as a little boy, "If the small quiet voice is speaking to you, you better listen." As I type, I ask the question, "In this modern world, did we lose the gift of our ancestors?" Are our minds so crammed with day to day irrelevant knowledge we can no longer hear? I think of my readings about Native American legends and their healing wisdom. Slowly, I come back to my original story and think enough has been said about the unidentified young men from Anna's picture box and the art of blowing out fire and healing wisdom.

My thoughts bring us back to Isaac and Martha's children. They all stayed in Alabama and had children of their own, except for Pearl. I knew each of Isaac's children from the time I was born until their deaths. I was part of these huge family gatherings under the trees. Nieces and nephews, and a large extended family would be scattered across the United States, traveling down other dusty roads and rutted trails. Somewhere, a fork in the road, with a decision to go right or left, carried them further away from Alabama. They wandered about until some settled out west in states like Texas, Kansas, California, and Oklahoma.

Many of the original Roberts family of Cleveland were Baptist. In Mother's picture box, she saved a newspaper clipping about the history of Cleveland Baptist Church. My family history was again connected to the founding of churches and their names listed as charter members. In the article, I recognized the names from 1893, W. B Roberts, Mr. & Mrs. J.M. Pass, Dora Roberts Blackmon, and Julia Roberts. These were names from James Isaac's family.

James Isaac and Martha Liberty Roberts (in center)

The best picture I have of the family shows James Isaac and Martha Liberty sitting in the middle of their children and grandchildren with the rest of family and friends scattered all around the front yard and under the shade trees, at a family get-together. These "get-togethers" continued into my childhood in warm weather with fresh blackberry pie, storytelling, and laughter. Time passed, life changed, and then, one day, they ended. Just over the treetops, the sun slowly went down on the family. Today, I am left wondering about Martha Liberty's role in the community as an old-fashion healer. With email and phone calls, pieces of the extended family come back together for me.

Isaac's siblings, children, nieces, nephews, and cousins created their own families and would not all be together again for years until the death of a family member who did not leave a will. That person was Isaac's brother, Arthur Roberts, who lived at the end of Tuscaloosa Road. Arthur's death brought the old Roberts family back to Blount County to meet and share a meal one more time under the shade trees at Myrtle Roberts Cornelius's home in Five Points, up the road from Cleveland.

In our modern world, kinfolks don't gather under shade trees much. We don't see the little puffs of dust rising as folks come to visit. Our shared family stories are lost to cell phones and computer games. As memories come back, there is an urgency to encourage others to write about their families and to take time to talk and visit, like the Roberts family of years ago.

Coffee, Sugar, and a Bit of Rationing

My day starts with my morning cup of coffee. It's a good idea to leave me alone until I've had a few minutes to get those first warm sips of that dark magic going down. There are always two extra bags on the shelf above the espresso maker. I grind my coffee beans for the rich flavor and amazing aroma. This is a product of which I never want to run out. It's hard to imagine going to the grocery store and not buying coffee. Some folks like a little sugar with this mysterious brew, and there are plenty of the white crystals on the shelves at Hometown Market.

In the bottom of one of Granny Anna's picture boxes, I found two old War Ration Books. I can't imagine why they were kept. Maybe, it was a reminder of what could happen on a national scale. From what I have read, nationwide food rationing started in the spring of 1942. Each member of the family was issued a ration book.

The Office of Price Administration (OPA) was in charge of rationing. There was a long, long list of items rationed: coffee, sugar, shoes, nylons, meats, fuel oil, gasoline, and household appliances. The idea behind rationing insured people could get their fair share. World War II and the war effort created importing problems. James Isaac

War Ration Books

Roberts was seventy-five when he received his War Ration Book Two.

The Book Two series was issued in January of 1943, while the Book Three series was issued in October of 1943. The OPA was finally disbanded in 1947. The modern value of these old books is not very much, but at the time of issue, they were a treasure. One of the posters I saw in my research has a woman with her hand raised in a pledge, "I pay no more than top legal prices. I accept no rationed goods without giving up ration stamps."

I grew up in a family who had seen the hard times war and rationing could bring. We were taught the value of food, good shoes, and, yes, coffee. We ate what was cooked and saved anything left for the next meal. An old family phrase comes back to me, "Waste not, want not." The old statement has been around since about 1772. My childhood was filled with the concept of "Waste not, want not." The other phrase which was often used was "You never know when you might need it." So, we canned and froze, never wasting food. We saved old fabric scraps, boxes, nails, twine, rusty tools, and the list goes on. This idea of rationing was silently passed down in my family. If it happened once, could it happen again? History repeats itself. There's another old saying that goes, "Those who don't learn history are doomed to repeat it."

Recently, I heard an advertisement on television about how much food is wasted each day in the United States. It seems a new generation never experienced those hard times. What would they do if they had to have a ration stamp for coffee, that favorite morning brew?

Droughts, Flash Floods, and Persistence

When I started writing my stories, Alabama was in a serious summer drought. Then, a year later, weeks with big raindrops fell and rivers overflowed. The showers started early in the morning with flash flood warnings across our state. It slowed me down to think about my year of typing. I hope I can help others know the value of persistence. That year taught me a lot about persistence and determination. If we have a story that keeps singing in our hearts and minds, we should take time to listen to that small voice singing, hear the words, and put them on paper.

Dora Roberts Blackmon with Isaac and Martha Roberts

Dora Roberts Blackmon, another child of W. B. Roberts, was a little known relative. A picture of her with Isaac and Martha Roberts on Tuscaloosa Road was one of those stories which began to sing to me. Her daughters, Lucille and Ida, showed up at Grandpa Albert's house about harvest time each year. Always dressed in their fine city clothes, they wouldn't pick anything to carry back to the big city of Birmingham. As we say, they were "dressed to the nines" for their trip to the country relations.

Our whole family worked on Grandpa's farm. We had big gardens with long rows of food for the winter months. We planted seeds saved from the previous year and sometimes bought something new if we could afford it. With the ground turned, we waited for the right day to put those little things in the soil. The perfect spring day came, and in the dirt, they would go. The waiting began for the warm Alabama sun to raise them up out of the dirt. We knew how to use a hoe to thin and space the growing plants. We also knew how to keep the weeds from going to seed. We knew how to dress for the fields. Everyone did their share of the picking and preparing, except for our 'city cousins.' They just appeared. There was some resentment by my daddy who often stated, "They just show up when the crops come in." And, Grandpa's reply was, "Well, Odell, they're family, and there's plenty to go round."

Ida Morrison (standing)
Lucille Hudson and Dora Blackmon

In Granny Anna's picture box, I found pictures of our city cousins, a newspaper clipping, and a letter from Ida I had not read. The family lost contact with each other after Lucille and Ida died. I remembered Lucille had only one son (Nolen), and Ida had no children. I couldn't remember anything else about Dora Roberts Blackmon. A newspaper article told me she was a Charter Member of First Baptist Church of Cleveland when it was organized in 1893. Her name was on the settlement documents for Uncle Arthur's estate in 1962. Here's where persistence comes in really handy. On that flooding morning, I read the letter Ida wrote to Mother. She told her about now living in Bay City, Michigan, a long way from Alabama. She was receiving good care from her nephew, Nolen, and his wife, Ann. Nolen was a doctor in Bay City, Michigan.

My clues about the family were few because I had not seen any of them since 1962. There were many internet searches, but I found a Nolen, Dr. Clayton Nolen Hudson. I read about the hospital where he worked as a breast cancer surgeon. It was a good day for writing letters to lost relatives, and so, I wrote a one page letter, addressing it to Dr.

Clayton Nolen Hudson at the hospital name I found. I briefly described who I was and for whom I was looking. As a good Southern lady, I thanked him and included my contact information, and simply stated, "If you are the Nolen I'm trying to find, I look forward to hearing from you." That's that, a stamp went on the envelope, and it went on its journey to Bay City. The Dora Roberts file went back in the drawer, and I moved on to another old picture.

Days and days went by; I put Dora to rest in that file. I suspected I would not get a reply, but I learned with research not to get disappointed if every clue does not yield usable information. One night, I was sitting in my recliner, trying to find something on television to interest me, when the phone rang. The voice said, "Is this Darnell, that's looking for Nolen?" Today, as I begin to type a story, I smile when I think of the word "persistence." Nolen thanked me for my persistence. This was the beginning of finding Nolen and Dora.

Years of living in the North had not taken the South out of Nolen. He was now in Mississippi, retired from the medical world. We began to share family information by e-mail, and one day a large package arrived from Mississippi. He shared the family research on Dora and the Blackmon family.

Dora came out of the file for this brief story. Her husband was M. C. Blackmon. Her children were Ercey, Brice, Therman, Ida, Lucille, Alda, and Whaley. I had only known the two girl cousins, Lucille and Ida. With permission from Nolen, I share a few short paragraphs.

It seems M. C. Blackmon was the type of relative who one would have to work hard to find good memories of, and then, put the rest away. Without asking the whys and whats of the information I learned, I found M. C. was on bad terms with his

M. C. Blackmon and One of His Daughters

children by the time they reached adulthood. His unwritten behavior alienated the sons to the point they changed the spelling of their last name, from Blackmon to Blackman. Lucille and Ida kept the Blackmon name.

Dora spent many years living with Lucille until a form of mental illness found its way to her. She spent her last days in Bryce Hospital in Tuscaloosa. When talking with Mom about Aunt Dora, she couldn't remember Dora being in Bryce, but we must think information may not have been shared with her. Mental illness was not something talked about during this period of time. She remembered Lucille said her mother was "hard to handle." Mom began to laugh, and a memory came back. "Dora would shake full Coca-Cola bottles, and then, run though the house spraying Cola."

Today, I put the Dora file away to rest in peace. Dora is buried in the old Forest Hill Cemetery in Birmingham. The advertisement for the cemetery states, "Forest Hill Cemetery, located in Jefferson County, Alabama, personifies the tradition of southern grace, charm, and beauty." I think of a little white house on First Avenue South in Birmingham, where Ida lived during my childhood. When I look at my three pictures of the family members, I smile as I recall my brother and I called them "the laughing people" when Ida and Lucille just showed up for fresh vegetables during harvest time.

The Benefit of Not Having a Will

There is a tombstone in Cleveland United Methodist Cemetery with the name of Arthur Roberts, my great-great-uncle who lived on Old Tuscaloosa Road. The dates of life are September 6, 1886, to December 23, 1961. Etched in stone are the words: Pvt U S Army, WWI Purple Heart. I knew him as a very eccentric, bright, educated person who kept to himself, never married, walked to the post office daily, and lived with a female cousin. He placed no trust in banks or the banking system of this country. A family story went: Perhaps, he lost money in the Great Depression of the 1930's. From then on, he put his money where he thought it would be safe, in the walls of his barn and house, under floor boards, and the out buildings on his farm. He bought land and a "Model T" to travel around the county. People who couldn't read and write got help from Arthur. But, with this ability to read and write, he never created his own will. Life passed, Arthur died. He left what some locals said was a common law wife. He also left a long list of relatives wanting a share of his estate.

While visiting with my mom, I told her I didn't have a story for Arthur who lived at the end of Tuscaloosa Road. Well, to clarify, she said he was 'short' Arthur. The other Arthur was her mom's brother, and this one was her granddaddy's brother. After World War I, Arthur went away to college at Auburn with plans of graduating. These plans ended when his father's wife got sick, and none of his siblings would care for her. To help Arthur with her personal care, he got Omie Horton, a distant cousin, to come and live at the Roberts home. (She is believed to be Jesse Horton's sister. Jesse Horton lived near my Grandpa Albert.) So, one story goes, Arthur came home to Cleveland, unhappy with the family because he couldn't finish his degree.

As I started typing my story, I thought about the death of Arthur's mother and was curious about the date she died. To my surprise, the death of Martha Jane Horton Roberts was May 29, 1887. Recorded in *People and Things from The Blount County News and Dispatch, 1879-1889,* "Near Anderton Ford, Blount County, Ala, the beloved wife of W.

B. Roberts, died of flux after an illness of about ten days." Something was wrong with my information somewhere. Arthur was born in 1886. So, the woman he cared for was not his biological mother, and here was another mystery from the past to figure out before finishing the story.

My Roberts file is thick with pages of information and lots of pictures of the family of William Bazzel Roberts. I felt a dread of more research, a "cold case" with no answers. Some days are blessed with clues, and then, sometimes weeks, even months go by without a reasonable answer. This day was a good day. In the front of the file was a gift from the past by an ancestor. My mother kept these three yellow pages entitled "Descendants of William Roberts." There were pages of his and Martha Jane Horton Roberts's children. Listed were James Isaac, Julia, Sarah, Dora, Joseph, C.L., and on the last page was William Arthur, born 1886. Below was an asterisk, and noted, second wife of William Roberts, Mary Jane Cornelius, born October 4, 1845, and died February 27, 1928, married after 1888. Thanks again to *People and Things from The Blount County News and Dispatch, 1879-1889,* I found dear old William Bazzel had married soon after his first wife died, "Near Anderton, Blount Co, Ala, on the 19th of January 1888, W. B. Roberts married Mary Jane Cornelius." His second wife raised his last child, but W. B. and Mary Jane had no children together. This added to the mystery of Arthur, and the story I wanted to write.

Finished with the clues about Arthur's dying step-mother, it was time to get back to the reason for the story and the connection to Tuscaloosa Road. Arthur never returned to Auburn, but stayed on after Mary Jane's death to be with his aging father. Arthur was well-know because of his help with the illiterate. Whether it was intentional, because of his early rift with his siblings, or an oversight, Arthur never wrote his own will. The disadvantage of this is clear to those who want to inherit as they wait on the court system to determine beneficiaries. It is an economical way to leave this life. Those left behind will deal with the expenses. Maybe, he finally attained revenge on his siblings for interfering with the Auburn degree he so desired.

Years passed, and sooner or later, we all die. Arthur died December 23, 1961, returning from his daily walk to the Cleveland Post Office. Joan Pass

Ellis lived with her family on the road Arthur took for his daily walk. She stated, "He dropped dead in front of us. I will never forget that day. He died instantly of a massive heart attack or stroke. He walked to the post office and was coming back. We always talked to him. I remember running in and screaming to Daddy something happened to Uncle Arthur."

He left behind 150 bushels of corn, one ton of hay, one 1928 Chevrolet automobile, farming tools, a house with furniture, barns, real estate, and money safely stored at home. His heirs were Miss Omie Horton and the children of his seven siblings. The news of Arthur's death was the talk of my small hometown for months, added to the questions about what would happen to Arthur's belongings. The fair inheritance was openly talked about among local relatives. This was a major event in my young life because the conversations in the family were many. It was legally decided there was no fair way to divide his estate and everything would be sold, and the money divided. We began to hear of relatives we had never met living in Texas, Oklahoma, Kansas, and even California.

The legal plans evolved to settle the estate of Arthur Roberts of Tuscaloosa Road.

At this point in Arthur's story, I stopped again. I need to explain to readers about this huge Roberts family. Some of my genealogy research would help, but I remembered only a few of the relatives who came from out of state. I found a picture of the lost relatives. It was made on the steps of the Blount County

Roberts Family at Settlement

Courthouse, dated March 1962.

In the bottom of the courthouse in Oneonta, there is a records room. It smells of old paper, and I had been only once before and really hadn't had much success. There was no major index. My best clue, the picture taken on the courthouse steps, and I were going to the basement one more time. I stopped at the museum for a little support for my research and was offered assistance from the curator with a phone call to the gentleman who worked in the records room. He was ready for me when I arrived, and I gave him the name of the deceased. The fellow disappeared up some stairs, and in a few minutes, reappeared with the most wonderful hole punched set of papers. Here was everything I needed to know about dear old Arthur's estate, the names of all his seven deceased siblings, the names of the twenty-eight heirs who would inherit, and Miss Omie Horton's right to inherit. It was a rich find, pages and pages of information, with the announcement from *The Southern Democrat,* published in April of 1962.

Arthur got his final revenge on the siblings who made him come home from Auburn. They never inherited, but their children did. Without a will, everything was sold in auction and divided. His sister, Dora Roberts Blackmon, was survived by five children. Lula Roberts Pass left behind four children. His brother, Joady, only had two children, but brother, Isaac, had an amazing seven. Sister, Sarah E. Roberts Logan, had five children who had moved out west to Kansas and Oklahoma. The last on the list was Julia Roberts Cornelius whose five children lived in Texas, Oklahoma, and California. Luckily, Miss Omie Horton received a fair inheritance.

The amazing event that came out of this was the last huge reunion of the Roberts family who once lived on Tuscaloosa Road. They visited in each other's homes around Blount County again. They all seemed to talk at one time. My brother and I were fascinated with all the laughter and conversations. They ate one big lunch together under the trees at the home of Taft Cornelius and his mother, Myrtle Roberts Cornelius, who lived in Five Points. All the women cooked, tables were set up by the men, white tablecloths appeared, and the food and relatives arrived. In my picture from that day, all heads were bowed in prayer as we met around the family table.

Dora Roberts Blackmon led the prayer. The edge of my Granny Anna's white hair could be seen, and my distant cousin from Oklahoma was standing near the porch.

There will always be a mystery surrounding the real reason Arthur left Auburn. After the inheritance checks were given out, goodbyes were made with promises of meeting again. The Roberts family would never meet again to share a prayer and a meal under the shade trees of Blount County.

Saying Grace
Roberts Family at Taft Cornelius Home

A Dapper Young Man - Another Arthur Roberts

Arthur A Roberts

For years, I was confused about the two Arthur Roberts in my family. Mom reminds me again with this picture, "There was long Arthur and short Arthur." That never helped much in the past: One was Anna Roberts's brother. The other Arthur was Isaac Roberts's brother, Anna's uncle, which only added to the confusion. My family was probably confused too, when talking about the two Arthurs, so the terms "long" and "short" were added to their names. In one of the inherited old picture boxes, I found a photograph of a very dapper man posed in front of a huge tree with his hand on his hip. That tree had been in other Roberts's pictures on Tuscaloosa Road. His tie was daring, I wish I knew the colors of the obviously lively flowers. With my notes in hand, I visited my mom to find out who the dapper fellow was.

This picture was of "long" Arthur, Anna's brother. Arthur Arnett Roberts was born on June 20, 1896. He married a lady named Stella but I have not found information about her. They are buried in Austin Creek Cemetery in the Blountsville area. I don't know why he wasn't buried with the other family members in Cleveland United Methodist Cemetery. He is the only Roberts family member we honor on Decoration Day at Austin Creek Cemetery. His grave is by the far left side of the cemetery, and we always put flowers out for him on the First Sunday in May.

Memories of this Arthur would not come to surface in my searching mind. Finally, I found the picture of his tombstone, and the question about my memory was answered. This ancestor died in 1950 when I was only five years old. I would never have memories of him, but Mom told me he lived with his mom and dad until their deaths.

Arthur A Roberts in Uniform

No stories have come my way about this Arthur, but I found another picture of him in his uniform and his military enlistment records. He served in the Great War, World War I. Mom said he never worked a regular job, and she believed he had a pension from the government.

As the morning fog flowed up covering my little hilltop home, I settled down at my table with my cup of coffee. I thought this would be a slow day for writing as there were no ideas ready to go on paper. My brain was an empty vessel. No words wanted to come out. Uncle Arthur's pictures lay there on the table. He seemed to be waiting for me so I sat with him for a while longer wishing for more information, more words, or a few simple phrases.

By the picture was a new book I purchased. The past Sunday, I heard the author, Nimrod Frazer, speak at a museum sponsored talk. His book, **Send the Alabamians,** and his discussion on World War I, renewed my interest in a period of history of which I knew very little. I loved the quote, "In time of war, send me all the Alabamians you can get, but in time of peace, for Lord's sake, send them to somebody else!" When I put the book down, I wondered about my ancestors who fought in the Great War. Robin Sterling's book, **Blount County, Alabama WWI Draft Card Abstracts**, was on the table. The last names of my ancestors filled his pages. How many would leave home for the first time to fight for someone else's freedom? There, by where I placed the book, was Uncle Arthur's picture. This morning's fog slowed me down and carried me away with images of foggy trenches created in my mind, as my Grandpa Albert would say, "across the great pond." On this gloomy morning, I thought about the sounds and smells of war, about young Alabamians leaving home. I could not be able to give enough praise or honor to my dead ancestors of long ago wars. I decorated the graves of family servicemen since childhood. I will look at those graves differently this Memorial Day.

Arthur mailed a letter to his sister, Anna Johnson, written from his bed in Tuscaloosa dated June 12, 1950. His spelling and grammar tells us about Arthur as he writes to her. It reads: "I am not doing any good I am in Bid {*sic*} most of the time. Don't never Expect to be any Better. Will have to spind {*sic*} the Rest of my days in the Bid. Pray for me ever time you pray." (Signed) Arthur A Roberts

Arthur would not return to Blount County to live. Mom said he died at the Veteran's Hospital in Tuscaloosa months after this last letter was written.

Wilburn Beavers told me about the day of Arthur's funeral. The ground was so hard the men folks couldn't use a shovel to dig. They worked all day, young and old men, but couldn't get the hole deep enough for the casket. Wilburn remembered, "It bothered us, he had to be taken back to the funeral home."

Thank goodness, these days we don't have to hand dig our loved one's graves.

Aunt Pearl Roberts

Special people should not be forgotten. Pearl Roberts, my grandmother's sister, is one of those people. Her name suggests she was a treasure, a pearl from the deep blue sea. She had a unique dialect, almost Old English. My love of flowers may have started with her. The old fashion petunias volunteered to grow in her unkempt yard. Sweet peas came back year after year to be with her. Wild violets and hollyhocks grew for her. Her sturdy independence and bright mind taught all of us so much about home and unhurried life.

Pearl was born on September 2, 1887. Pearl and I had many conversations, but she never talked about deceased family members. We talked about current news. I often wish I asked her about her memories of these people when I was a young girl. In that long ago time, I didn't know to ask about them. She had stories about vanished ancestors.

Pearl Roberts

She spent her days in and around the house build by her father on Old Tuscaloosa Road. After her mother and daddy died, Pearl continued to live in the old Roberts's home. She never married as her sweetheart died when she was very young. There was never another man in her life. During my childhood, I didn't know about the boyfriend who died. I would have sat quietly and listened to her stories of him and how they met. Mom stated when someone came to tell Pearl he died, she simply said, "I already know." How and why he died is a mystery. Whatever her hopes and dreams were, they ended. She became our "old maid" aunt, oblivious to the changing world beyond her homeplace.

For a few months after her high school graduation, Uncle Dewey's daughter, Frances, lived with Aunt Pearl. Frances worked at Elmore's 5 &

10 in Oneonta. She recalls the lack of electricity, no indoor restroom, no running water, and cold rooms when winter came. She remembered Aunt Pearl went to college in Blount Springs, but no one in the family knows the college's name.

Aunt Pearl Roberts

Aunt Pearl lived the life of a true hermit. Her surroundings were homely and commonplace. Bare wood floors and walls remained as her parents left them. The furniture, old and gray, stayed in the same place year after year. She never had a telephone, television, refrigerator, or indoor plumbing. There were never electric lights, but I do remember oil lamps. The well she drank her water from was on a back porch. A bucket and dipper sat on a low shelf nearby. She had a battery radio and listened to the news throughout the day. Being a hermit didn't mean she wasn't interested in the outside world, she simply didn't want to participate in the world. Her radio gave her as much of mankind as she needed.

Her only income was a small social security check which came in the mail each month. She did not go to a grocery store. She put a list in an envelope with money in the mailbox for the mail carrier to deliver to the store in Cleveland. Delivered groceries arrived on her front porch by whoever came her way. If she wanted stamps, she left the money with a note in the mailbox.

Growing up next door to Aunt Pearl meant I checked on her health and well being, making a short walk up Tuscaloosa Road. As the weather warmed each year, the petunias and sweet peas greeted me. She swept a small area of the yard with a straw broom, so no grass grew. On the front porch of the aging house, I spent a lot of time in conversation with her about current events, things she heard about on the radio. Many times, she questioned something she heard on a recent radio broadcast. I felt wise and worldly to be able to clarify a news event or add some information. I became interested in world news at an early age because of our conversations. When the weather turned cold, we sat in two chairs in front of a small fire built in the parlor fireplace. The house was cold and drafty, as currents of cold air flowed inside, but she refused to leave her home of many years.

    What I loved the most about our time together was her taking the time to listen to me. She enjoyed my company. We were girls together having conversation about life beyond our road. I look back at the simple life of this lovely Southern woman with amazement. By today's standards, she lived in poverty. By her standards, she lived in peace with her family memories and her radio. Pearl suffered a stroke and spent her last years in a nursing home in Oneonta. She died on December 6, 1975. She is buried in the Cleveland United Methodist Church Cemetery, resting in a long line of Roberts's family tombstones. This simple, amazing life she was part of slowly vanished, along with the Roberts home, but they are not forgotten.

Uncle Has a Moment

T. C. and Jewel Roberts with Webster

Of all my Granny Anna's brothers and sisters, Uncle T. C. was the one of whom I have the most outstanding memories. I don't remember him for his calm, quiet, loving ways. I remember him for the wild enthusiasm he had for life and with everyone he came in contact. We kindly said Uncle T.C. was a real character! Adding to this "character," the family used three different names when referring to him - TC, T.C. and Tessie. When going through my mom's and Granny's picture boxes, I found more pictures of Uncle T.C. than any other relative.

He left Blount County as a young man and lived in Birmingham. During my childhood, he lived in a neat little white house on a hill overlooking the Birmingham Airport. Some weekends, we visited him and Aunt Jewel at their home on the hill. My memories are of a well kept city lawn and a view of the Birmingham Airport. We watched the amazing 'Air Shows' from his house and heard the roar of airplanes.

He visited his Blount County kinfolks several times a year. When he came to Cleveland, I wanted to hide under the bed. He was tall and skinny, loud and unpredictable in my young opinion. He grabbed my Granny Anna, swung her around and around and laughed much too loudly for my comfort. When he finished with her, Mom was next, and by that time, I looked for a place to hide. Grandpa Albert would just step aside and watch. He may have wanted a place to hide. After all the joyful swinging folks around, he slowly settled into a family visit.

Jewel Moffitt became his wife. She was so soft spoken and calm, a pleasant Southern lady. She was a native of Birmingham. I always wondered what dynamics bought the two together. They had two children,

Webster and Mary Ann. He retired from a job near his home while the city of Birmingham developed many of the interstates and one way streets.

My favorite story of Uncle T.C. was his Sunday morning trip to try out one of the new interstate highways. After his retirement, he used the old streets he knew for short trips around his neighborhood. He knew Birmingham very well after spending his adult life there. Early Sunday morning, he told Aunt Jewel he was going for a drive and would be back in few minutes. Time passed, and Aunt Jewel became very worried when he didn't return. She checked with people he might have gone to visit, and no one had seen T.C. Sometime later, he returned with the announcement he would never drive "those damn roads" again. He became lost in Birmingham. He laughed when he told the story, adding some interesting comments, in words and ways only Uncle T.C. could do. He went back to using those old familiar streets and left the changes to a new generation.

At seventy-two, I still drive into the Birmingham areas, I think of him often when I experience Highway 280 and Interstate 459. I drove these areas for around forty years, and some days, I have what I call an "Uncle T.C. moment." Am I lost in Birmingham, a city I knew all my adult life? I look for old landmarks and old streets, as he perhaps did that morning he got lost in his hometown. Thinking about Uncle T.C., I figure out where I am, as he probably did that morning long ago, smile, and make my way back to Blount County.

Frances Darnell Whited

Finding Uncle Dewey

Uncle Dewey Roberts

Many times, I've said to myself, "You can only chase one rabbit at a time." Isaac Roberts had eight children. That's a lot of rabbits to chase around Blount County and beyond. Granny Anna had several pictures of her brother, Dewey, another of Isaac's children. In his pictures, I see reflections of my granny and me. Spreading these old photographs across the table, I realized we three have those skinny arms and legs. We have what I call a "raw bone look" with a sharp bony nose, eyes a little deep in the sockets, and very pronounced cheekbones. Thank goodness, and genetics, I didn't get those Roberts's ears.

Uncle Dewey was born on June 2, 1898. He had a large family of his own and lived in the Blountsville area, almost in Garden City. Many of his children were still alive, and finding Uncle Dewey's children became one more rabbit I intended to chase around the county.

It was a wonderful Saturday visit to Uncle Dewey's daughter, Eula Jean (Roberts) Copeland's house that started it all! It was my hope to find more pictures. After that visit, Jean and I began to talk on the phone, and I told her I would love to bring Mom to see everyone for one last time. Mom's mobility was really getting worse, and I felt a need to do this soon. Maybe, we could meet at a restaurant in Cullman.

The old Roberts's genetics for get-togethers must have surfaced in all of us. The plan came to fruition with everyone journeying to the Vinemont home of Sarah Roberts Miller. Dewey's daughters: Sarah, Virginia, Rena, Eula Jean, and Frances were all there. Frank, the only son, died years before. Fourteen of Isaac Roberts's descendants came together with a spread of food that flowed across the kitchen. He would have been amazed at what happened. A spontaneous conversation started, the memories came back, and the stories began. The smell of food filled the air. Sweet iced tea was there.

I sat on a stool and watched the tradition of family get-togethers come alive. Laughter came from all directions. Several people talked at one time. Time came to bless the food. The family circle was formed. With fourteen folks holding hands around the kitchen, Carol Hayes (Uncle Dewey's granddaughter) blessed the food. In 2017, I found Uncle Dewey and the sweet charm of Southern family life in Vinemont, Alabama.

Of course, I wanted a story about Uncle Dewey. "Ok, folks, I need a funny story about Uncle Dewey." That started the conversation in several directions. "He was quiet, didn't have a lot to say." I waited for the words to put to paper, and then, it happened. Frances, who lived with Aunt Pearl for a while, remembered saving her money to buy a car while she worked at Elmore's 5 & 10 in Oneonta. The word "car" was all I needed.

And the story goes: "Daddy drove a car, but he never had a license. He had a straight shift, and he never could get it in gear. He drove all his life without a license and could never hit second gear. We rode with him and said 'Jump us, Pa', as he missed second gear one more time. And, when he left home, he started the car at the top of hill and never slowed down as he drove onto the highway. He drove on down the road. We put in a dollar's worth of gas and filled up with oil. Mr. Bullard pushed us off when the car wouldn't start, and the bumpers caught together. Once a year, we made the trip to pay Mr. Green the house payment. He was related to Grandma Green." The girls smiled, when someone said, "We loved to rub Daddy's bald head. He said the measles got his hair!"

Sitting in front of my computer screen, I drift back in time to the Roberts homeplace on Tuscaloosa Road. I look over at the picture of that huge family gathered around Isaac and Martha. I imagine Martha giving Dewey's children chewing gum, a very special treat in those days. They would be happy to know the family went on after them and still had get-togethers.

Uncle Dewey and his wife, Verna Mae, are buried in the little cemetery called Mt. Tabor. It's located at the end of a dusty road in what locals call the Gum Springs area. Frank rests near his parents. A little further down is Dewey's sister, Etta Belle and her family. On a windy

Saturday, I walked the rows of graves at Mt. Tabor and felt the tranquility all around me. There's no church, only an entrance arch and the rows of tombstones. I sat on the bench engraved with "Roberts." It's a peaceful Blount County cove surrounded by mountains and trees, a quiet place to complete a journey.

Dewey Roberts Family

Aunt Etta Belle and Visiting Relatives

In the 1950's and 60's, one thing my brother and I were always assured of was visiting relatives. The conversation would start with, "We haven't heard from (fill in the name of the relative here). We need to go check on them." Remember, in those days, there were no telephones, internet, or texting. Those came years in the future. Letters were the main means of communication, along with travelers passing from place to place. On this particular day, Mom said, "We haven't heard from Aunt Etta Belle lately." They decided to go for a visit.

We loaded the car with Mom, Dad, Granny Anna (Etta Belle's sister), Grandpa Albert, my brother, and me. There were conversations on the drive from Tuscaloosa Road on to Blountsville and out into the countryside. Daddy and Grandpa sat in the front seat with Daddy driving. As a child, it seemed like a long, long drive, but the stories and conversation of the adults made the journey worthwhile. Sometimes, my brother and I crawled into the front seat. No one wanted us to get carsick and ruin the day, the car, or anyone sitting near us. Car sickness was a terrible thing.

Blountsville was a real town, bigger than Cleveland, and this was because it had a movie theater. I always waited for the theater to appear on my right. We went to see a movie one time with Mom and Dad. The building filled with people, and the big screen was amazing. Sounds filled the room. Did they sell popcorn? I've tried hard to remember the name of the movie, but the information never surfaces. Jesse James and Bonnie and Clyde are names from the period, but whatever the movie, it was a crowd pleaser and a success in my young mind.

Imogene, Allie, Etta Belle and Mary

Blountsville had beautiful two-story Southern homes and charming old churches. At some point, one of these houses became Dr. Sutton's office. My Aunt Villa gave birth to one of her babies there. My brother and I waited outside, and we waved to her at the window. There were no stop signs or red-lights in the Blountsville of my youth. The car driver used common sense when driving into town and took a left turn past the theater to go out of town to my relatives. Then, the longest part of the drive started because there wasn't much to see. But, the stories always began. We learned about Davy Crocket, who probably traveled into Blountsville. Grandpa told us about the field with the bottomless spring. We saw it on the right. The grass was always green and tall. Today, there is a water treatment plant for Blountsville near the location, and the legend of the bottomless spring is still alive. Daddy told about the other spring with a bottom where it was safe to stop for water. We passed the Ratliff Store and Warren Ratliff's house. They must be rich people.

Aunt Etta Belle was born in 1901 and married Allie K. Burgess. They lived in a magnificent white two-story house. Jerry and I were on our best behavior at this quiet home between the mountains. There were no other houses to be seen, and I don't remember playing in the carefully maintained yard. Mom told me to take care of my little brother while the adults talked. Jerry and I were always polite. Adults visited on these trips.

Mom remembered Aunt Etta Belle often wore a scarf over her head, tied under her neck, when she went away from home. Mom said she had a "wen." What, I asked, was a wen? I never heard the word used. "Well, it's like a boil." Another word we seldom hear used these days is "boil." We believe this to be what is now called a tumor. It grew on her neck for some time, and she wouldn't go to the doctor. The family feared it might be cancer. Someone convinced her to make the trip to Cleveland to see Dr. Brown. He wouldn't do the surgery in Cleveland so Etta Belle made the long trip to Birmingham. The surgery was a success, no cancer, and she returned to Gum Springs.

Mother's use of the word "wen" sent me in search of the word's origin. It seems it may be Old English and beyond, Low German. Throughout my life, I heard many words used by my family indicating their language was passed down, not influenced by changes in modern language. This language from the past makes for another interesting story about our dialect, strange words, and idioms.

A few weeks back, I drove past Aunt Etta Bella's old homeplace. I took a sentimental journey back in time as I roamed the old Blount County road. Not much changed since the day trip with my family. Mt. Tabor Church was still on the left. Uncle Dewey's place was a short drive on past Etta Belle's stately home. His little house was still there, remodeled by a family member. On my way back to my hilltop home, I wondered if parents still loaded the family for a day trip to relatives. Do they tell the stories they were told as they ramble along a back road? I've noticed a lot of anger in the world. It's hard to be angry when you're telling tales from your family's past.

Frances Darnell Whited

Aunt Eula Holt of Sugar Creek

The picture of Aunt Eula and baby, Annie Ruth, was forgotten. There are so many pictures to sort and connect with a family story. Eula Roberts Holt was almost overlooked. While looking for another picture, there she was in the bottom of a box. She was a fun person to be with, happy, but not in the wild way of her brother, Uncle T. C. Why had I forgotten her? I put the blame on too many pictures and not enough words.

She lived in a large unpainted house down at Sugar Creek. It had a long porch which ran across the front of the house with lots of

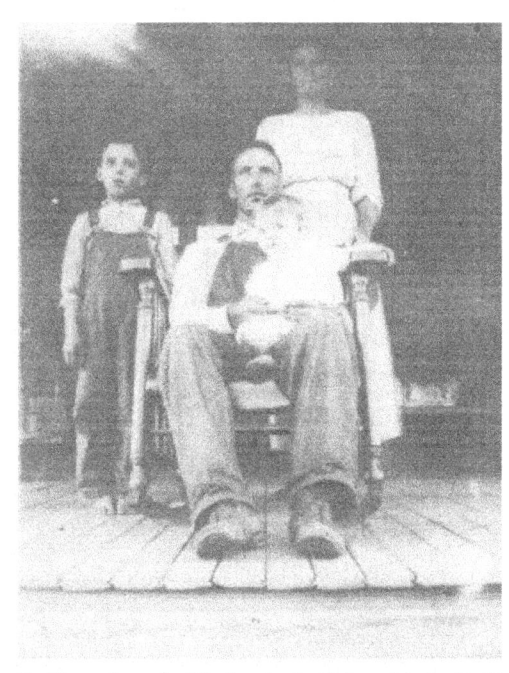

Erskine, Sam (with Annie Ruth) and Lula Holt

chairs. We drove on past Nectar to visit her and Uncle Sam. Her daughter, Annie Ruth, and Mom were good friends. In later years, Annie Ruth and her husband, Sidney Bellenger, bought the old Isaac Roberts's homeplace next door to Mom where they built a new, modern home.

I sat talking with Mom on Thanksgiving Day and told her I needed a funny story about Aunt Eula. "Well, I can't remember one about her, but I can tell you one about her son, Erskine. Mama always liked visiting Aunt Eula and spending the night. Erskine wanted a red bird really badly. He built a trap when Mama spent the night. The next day Erskine left for school, and Mama decided to make a false bird. She found some old cloth and made a bird. She put it in the trap and closed the door. When Erskine came home from school, he checked his trap. 'I caught a bird! I caught a bird!' Then, he opened the door and found the old cloth bird. 'I don't know who done this, but I think it was Aunt Anna.' He knew she liked to play games." When she was feeling healthy, Granny Anna was a lot like

Uncle T.C., full of mischief. Mom settled back in her chair and laughed, "I miss all those people."

Aunt Myrtle of Five Points

Anna & Myrtle at Anna's Home on Tuscaloosa Road

Myrtle Roberts of Tuscaloosa Road met and married Lonnie Cornelius of Five Points, Alabama. By horse and buggy, Five Points was a dusty four miles from Cleveland. Somewhere back in time, there was a spot where five roads met and led on in five different directions. Five Points got its name. One of the early families who settled in this community was the Cornelius family. The Cornelius name is well known in old Blount County. The cemeteries of Five Points are filled with the family member's graves.

The Heritage of Blount County, Alabama, states about Five Points, "Around 1900 to 1940, Zion Cornelius operated a saw mill and grist mill. Other early businesses included a sawmill operated on Clyde Cornelius' farm…a blacksmith shop operated by Oscar Cornelius." Myrtle's marriage to a Cornelius gave her a respected place in the community. She and her husband built a very nice home, painted white with a porch all the way across the front. It was much bigger than my Granny Anna's house. As a child, I wanted a house that looked like the home of Aunt Myrtle and Uncle Lonnie.

Searching for Lonnie's ancestors became a bit confusing. There are books about the history of Cornelius family in the museum. One cold day, after another confusing search, I decided since Lonnie Cornelius was a genealogical matter, I would put it aside for later. The story went on without his parents' names, without his connection to a childhood friend, and with questions about Zion and Mittie Cornelius unanswered. My curiosity would be satisfied with the knowledge Miles Horton Cornelius and Clyde Cornelius were brothers, and Lonnie was related, but not documented by me.

As I often do, I asked Mom for a story from her memory. Mom loves her stories and is always happy to share another. She began, "Aunt Myrtle was another sister who your Granny Anna liked to visit overnight. There was Decoration Day coming up, and she went to Five Points to spend the night with Lonnie and Myrtle. She planned to go with them the next day. That morning everyone was up, finished with breakfast, and dressed for the day. Lonnie announced the rats ate a hole in his Sunday pants. It wasn't a small hole, and it couldn't be fixed. He didn't go to Decoration that day. They went to church without him."

Mom remembers, "Taft, Myrtle's son, was always a lot of fun." Laughing, she said, "One day, he put a possum in Mama's mailbox. Mama called Odell to come get the possum. He carried it up to Jay and Zinkie Bryan. They cooked it with sweet potatoes and onions in a big pot. You know, people ate possum back then. I didn't cook possum." My memories of Taft are rather simple. He was always happy and smiled a lot. He had a barber shop beside his mother's house. Sometimes, Dad and Jerry got haircuts there. Mom took a picture of David, Taft's son, and me in a wheelbarrow when we were children.

From Cleveland, if you drive very slowly up Five Points Road, Taft's old barber shop is still there on the left. The old house I loved is replaced with a more modern home. Today, as I type, I think I'm like my mom. I miss those simple family times.

Taft Cornelius's Barber Shop, 2018

Frances Darnell Whited

The Good Country Doctor[1]

Dr. Eldridge Tracy Brown

Mr. Tracy Brown's classic, old Southern home no longer exists, but as one drives down Highway 231 into Cleveland, the huge magnolia trees remain on the left side of the road. He is remembered for his Model T car and his son, Dr. Eldridge Tracy Brown. Eldridge Bynum wrote about the doctors of Cleveland, but Dr. Brown was the country doctor remembered by older local families.

Why am I including Dr. Brown with the Roberts family? A simple reason. Mom told the story Dr. Brown grew up around the Roberts family of Tuscaloosa Road. Her grandmother, Martha Roberts, took care of him when his own mother was unable to care for her baby boy. Was she what was commonly called a "wet nurse"? Historically, a wet nurse refers to "a woman who breast feeds and cares for another's child. Wet nurses are employed when the mother is unable or elects not to nurse the child herself." Martha's son, Arthur, and Tracy were born the same year. Around the family at an early age, Eldridge Tracy said he wanted to be a doctor. During his life, he often visited the Roberts family like they were his kin.

Dr. Brown's office was in the center of Cleveland, next door to the Blackwood garage building, which still stands. He kept a supply of medications and filled his own prescriptions. My mom worked part-time for him. She recalled her duties: answering the phone and working in the "drug store." She sold a special tonic and a salve for impetigo without a

---

[1] ***The Heritage of Blount County, Alabama, Vol. 5****, p. 131, has a brief account of Dr. Brown but doesn't mention the personal caring side of this country doctor. There's another account in **Alabama's Blount County Physicians** published by the Blount County Medical Auxiliary, 1984, which has more information, as well as a wonderful picture of him with that mischievous grin and carnation in his lapel.*

prescription. Impetigo was a common skin disease in the 1940's and 50's. Bacteria loved the humid Alabama weather, reused towels, and passed easily from person to person.

Babies were born at home, back then, delivered by Dr. Brown. House calls were a common practice in those days. My brother was born in the Cleveland clinic. Later, kicking and screaming with a terribly high fever, the doctor visited. Jerry was diagnosed with tonsillitis in the family kitchen. Mom, to this day, says, "Well, Dr. Brown said…" and the conversation moves to the advice given by the country doctor who made house calls. To Mom, his words are as good today as they were then.

A friend and classmate, Jerry Cornelius, of Five Points, told me he was born at home, delivered by Dr. Brown. He told the family, "This little fellow needs a middle name: It can be Brown," and so, Jerry Brown Cornelius was named for Dr. Brown. We often wondered, "How many other babies share the middle name of Brown around Blount County in his honor?" After talking with another Blount Countian and pastor, W. C. Green, he recalled all seven children in his family were probably delivered at home by Dr. Brown. W. C. told of one delivery when his mom had a "hard time," and Dr. Brown stayed the night in the home until he felt she was doing well enough for him to leave.

One day, as I sat with Mom and Jeanette Sherrer, they looked at my picture of Dr. Brown. Both had a lot of stories about this dear Southern doctor and his caring ways. Jeanette shared a wonderful story about the day her mother, Vera Ridgeway, died. Dr. Brown came to the house and stayed by her bedside until the end. He held Vera's hand and comforted Jeanette as they waited for the passing.

Dr. Brown was born on January 20, 1896, and died December 10, 1956. His tombstone reads "Physician & Surgeon." He saw so many changes in medicine, visited so many homes, but most importantly, he knew his patients. Can we say that about our doctors in this modern world? Do they know their patients as well as Dr. Brown did? Sometimes, when I go for my medical check-ups with Dr. Manes in Cleveland, I stop at the cemetery and walk slowly around all these folks from my past. I like where Dr. Brown's grave is located with the community all around him and the Roberts family nearby. Maybe, he's still taking care of these folks in his own special way.

(Photograph Courtesy of the Blount County Memorial Museum)

The above picture is the childhood home of Dr. Eldridge Tracy Brown. Note the unpaved road in front of the house. It will one day become Highway 231.

Chapter 3 - Footprints of the Johnson Family

We started out on the dusty Old Tuscaloosa Road of the Roberts family of Cleveland. We will leave them farming and drift further south in Blount County and find the Johnson family in Guinn's Cove. Joel Johnson came down from Tennessee in search of a young girl he planned to marry. The certainty and uncertainty of traveling to Alabama over unpaved roads with few directions did not deter Joel. Maybe, he followed the old Tennessee Trail to another old trail and passed Bear Meat Cabin. I can't document this, but I vision him leaving the life he knew, following the trails between the hills and mountains, bouncing along the dusty roads that led south. Did he have what some historians called "Alabama Fever?"

Darnell's drawing of Bear Meat Cabin

Frances Darnell Whited

Albert and Anna (Roberts) Johnson Family

This may be stating an obvious point, but as travelers delving into the past, if the people are to be perceived as real, we must meet them in their place in history. We'll view again their paths to Alabama, and see them in the clothes of their time. We will ponder the dangers of their journey and only guess at the rising rivers they had to cross. The cold, the hot, the rain, the snow...all these elements were just part of the trip, to be endured to reach the place where the grass touched a horse's belly. We have to take into account the happenings of their times, as that influenced how they lived and loved.

Most of my family farmed the fields. The ancestors of Albert and Anna (Roberts) Johnson were colorful people, full of character and adventure. At night, stories of wagon trains, bad crops, black panthers carrying off small children, the Civil War, and other tales were handed down as oral history. Much of what was shared in stories was true, despite not being written down. With the help of census records, family Bibles, and wills, we found corroboration of some of the written history and facts about Albert and Anna which can be established.

(Front) Albert (with hat), Darnell, Martha (holding Jerry)
(Back) Anna, Bud, Norman, Villa, Charles

Albert and Anna had three children: Martha Frances (June 23, 1923), James Henry (April 6, 1926-April 5, 1977), and Charles (March18, 1933 - January 31, 1957). James Henry "Bud" married Norma Gilliland. They had no children. Charles married Villa Dell McHan, and they had two children, Valerie and Charlotte.

Martha Frances married Odell Grigsby (April 8, 1919-January 9, 2003). Odell is buried in Westside Baptist Cemetery in Cleveland, Alabama. They had two children, Frances Darnell and Jerry Lynn (February 10, 1949-December 1, 2016). Darnell Grigsby married Budd Alston Rainey. They had one child, Bart Alston Rainey. Darnell married a second time to Phillip Whited, but they had no children. Jerry Grigsby married Linda Hamrick, and they had one child, Anthony Grigsby.

Frances Darnell Whited

Bent Nails

In 2016, the Blount County Memorial Museum in Oneonta, hosted a book talk by author Ryan Cole who wrote **Bangor: Days Gone By**, a book I had not read and didn't own. Growing up, I heard stories of Bangor and Bangor Cave from my daddy and Grandpa Albert. I walked the weedy, overgrown road more than once to see the inside of the famous cave. Daddy always led the way down the path, and every visit felt like the first, always a new adventure. The cave came alive to my brother and me as we explored the cool, damp cavern, with its mossy rock bar and earthy smells. We listened as Mom and Dad talked about the stories they knew, and we imagined the forbidden activities in this strange place. It had been a "speakeasy." Sometimes, it was advertised as the underground night club in the South. Bangor had a train station so folks arrived from all over to the mysterious place. It was said it had lots of lights that twinkled among the stalactites. My brother and I almost heard the laughter echoing in the dark spaces. Did we hear a train whistle?

I decided to buy my own copy of Mr. Cole's book and spend some time with his words and old pictures. To my surprise, page seven of the book gave me another insight to my Grandpa Albert Johnson's family. At best, I only hoped to refresh my memories of Bangor Cave.

Here was information about Joel Johnson's early years. Joel Johnson was born around 1795, in North Carolina. According to family history, Joel told his brothers he was going to Blount County to wed Mary (Polly) Elliot, whom he knew in North Carolina. He found Mary in Alabama and married her around 1818. They settled in the eastern part of what we call McAnnally Cove. Joel owned the land that became known as Johnson Point, the peak of the mountain which borders the east side of McAnnally Cove. Joel and Mary had nine

Joel Johnson, Jr

children. After Mary's death, Joel married again to Sarah Cullwell, whose maiden name was spelled many ways. Joel's family continued to grow with the birth of eight more children. One son, James Henry, married Frances E. McGuire around 1883. Their son, Albert, married a tall skinny girl from Old Tuscaloosa Road named Anna Roberts. *The Heritage of Blount County, Alabama, Vol. 5* includes many articles about the Johnson family.

James Albert, my grandpa, never told me about his Grandpa Joel. There is a strong possibility Joel's family knew the Methodist preacher, Charles Guynn, who preached in the area of Blount Springs. The reference in Mr. Cole's book has quotes from Mary Gordon Duffee's, *Sketches of Blount County, Alabama.* Duffee wrote of the preacher and the "picturesque spot" of Guynn's Cove (now spelled Guinn's). Many of Joel's family are buried in the cove. Some of the Johnsons moved from the Gwinn's Cove area, and their son, James Henry, settled in the Moss Bridge area to raise a large family.

Grandpa Albert was most likely strongly influenced by the settlers of Guinn's Cove. He was a calm, peaceful, God-loving man. He read his Bible every night in front of the fireplace. His level of education made reading the King James Version of the "Good Book" very hard for him. His strict interpretation of the written word made for interesting conversations. If the "Good Book" said there were "four corners of the earth," there <u>were</u> four corners, and we just hadn't found those corners yet! These conversations endeared him to me, and I learned not to challenge my grandpa's understanding of the "Good Book." Each day, he said his morning prayer, on his knees, in the big old barn behind his house. After he died, my mother showed me the spot in the dirt where he prayed. Years of kneeling in the same place created a solid, compacted imprint of his humble position.

For Albert Johnson, there was never much money. As we sometimes say in the South, he 'grew up hard.' He was raised in a house full of kids, brothers and sisters. I remember hearing the names of his brothers: Ace, Laney, Clint and Alvin. There is a long line of graves at Green's Chapel Cemetery with Johnson names. Mother told me many times of his siblings who died in the flu pandemic from 1918 to 1919.

Grandpa learned a strong work ethic and sound economic principles. He cut wood year 'round to burn in Granny's wood burning stove. If you wanted to build something in Grandpa's days, you didn't find a construction company. Instead, you found as many able-bodied family members and neighbors as you could get, your construction crew. Wasting supplies was almost considered a sin against God. If you dropped a nail, you picked it up. It went back in the nail bucket. According to Grandpa, if you bent a nail, it was to be picked up and put in a different bucket.

My grandpa never used a "bad" word. His strongest profanity was "Ah, Pshaw!" I didn't know what the word "Pshaw" meant, but if Grandpa used it, we knew he was unhappy[2].

My daddy had a building project on Old Tuscaloosa Road, and nails were dropped. Nails were expensive and couldn't be wasted lying on the ground. Daddy assigned me the job of picking up the dropped nails. I was very proud of my bucket filling up and showed him. He told me to pick out the bent nails because he couldn't use them. Grandpa heard this and with an "Ah, Pshaw, Odell," he told me to save those bent nails. When winter came, he would straighten them. Daddy didn't have time to straighten nails, but he let me save the bent nails for Grandpa. And, when winter came, Grandpa sat in his straight back, wooden fireplace chair, dipped snuff, and straightened nails for the spring.

---

[2] The expletive "Pshaw" dates from 1607 and generally is used to express irritation, disapproval, contempt, or disbelief.

Hot Days and Johnson Ancestors

Next to finding old tales about long dead ancestors, gardening is my favorite pastime. On a June day, I rolled out of bed at 5:30 to beat the heat of the hot summer day. It was a cool, cloudy day, and my young helper was at my house by 6:30 a.m. We got busy with our projects. All the birds were angry because we were in their territory. ***The Blount Countian*** recently wrote an article about my Monarch project. These beautiful butterflies are endangered. I enjoyed a brief moment of pride in the art of gardening. I thought about a picture album on the dining room table, borrowed from Patrick Fendley of the Oneonta Coin Exchange. Patrick and I have shared ancestors, Joel Johnson and Joel's dad, Lewis Johnson. Patrick is descended from Joel's first wife, and I am descended from the second wife. While I was gardening, the borrowed album passed in and out of my thoughts. Dirt and irises were flying everywhere, and Lucus Butts, my helper, moved rocks to line my milkweed beds. Around eleven o'clock, I realized I had been in the yard longer than my seventy-two year-old body probably needed for one day. As we put up tools for the morning, I again thought of the album and the trust Patrick had in me to keep it safe and return it in a timely matter.

After I showered the dirt, chiggers (those tiny red insects), and ticks off, I had an ounce of energy for the trip to return the album to Patrick. Really, some things are meant to be. I could have stayed home in the cool air but decided to run a few errands in Oneonta. After all, I wasn't going by horse and buggy into town from out on the mountain. I could make the trip in a few minutes in an air-conditioned vehicle! Sometimes, after searching for ancestors and living with old pictures, I forget about all the conveniences of the modern world, which I kindly refer to as modern mayhem!

Patrick smiled when I entered the store, and I thought he had a paying customer. I came in quietly, not to interfere with a possible coin sale with the lady. As I said, some things are meant to be. It was not a customer, but the lady was Nancy Johnson, a relative I never met. Patrick gave me her name and phone number, and the note disappeared into some file folder for later. An old phrase came back to me, "better sooner than later."

Frances Darnell Whited

Nancy searched for lost Johnson ancestors for many years and knew all about Joel and Lewis Johnson.

Stories of the Johnsons from years ago began to flow. I admit, a person must have a real passion for finding these old dead folks to enjoy this stuff and think it's a great day when you make a connection. Some people, bored beyond words and reason, would find no interest in the long dead. I was so pleased my energy survived the morning, and I talked to others with the same passion and interest.

Nancy told me a delightful story of Joel's second wife, Sarah Culwell (Cullwell). So, the story goes: In her declining years, Sarah went, as we on occasion say, "a little crazy." It seems everyone knew Sarah had a few mental issues, but, in those days, there was no trip to the psychologist. You took care of your own folks the best you could. The family and extended family lived in Guinn's Cove at the time. One day, Joel's brother and his wife washed clothes at the river near the foot of the mountain. They carried the wash pot with them. Suddenly, rocks flew off the ridge above, hitting the pot with a loud noise. They called to Sarah, "Sarah, stop throwing those rocks! You're going to hit the pot and crack it." Her reply, "I ain't trying to hit your damn pot! I'm trying to hit you!" We love oral history with the favor of life. We only assume before the mental issue took over, Sarah was a polite Southern lady with sweet Southern charm.

Nancy and Patrick told me about the Johnson reunion in Iuka, Mississippi, and another reunion for Johnsons, which usually happens in April of each year. I put a note on my calendar to forward to next year, "Check on Johnson reunions." Who knows what stories could float up to the surface from our far-away past?

Shortly after that visit, I received a letter from Sarah Roberts Miller. She told me about a church friend who was related to Joel Johnson.

Jean Mummert and Martha Frances Grigsby

Her friend, Jean Mummert, is from Hanceville. This began another journey into the past with a detailed visit to a descendant of Joel Johnson. By fate or the powers that be, we found a direct descendant of mother's beloved Aunt Bet Price. We heard Elizabeth "Bet" Price was probably buried in Graves Cemetery in Royal, Alabama. I drove by it for years on my way to a friend's house on Hamilton Mountain Road. Many times, I stopped and thought about walking around, but then, drove on, because I thought I had no connections to the families on that old road.

Today, as a soft cool breeze comes in from the north, I despair. I think I will never be able to write it all down in an accurate, readable, interesting way. Again, I ask, will anyone care about these old folks of Blount County's dusty roads?

Frances Darnell Whited

A Pause for Joel Johnson

In that moment of questioning and despair, I think a pause for Joel Johnson is needed. My file for Joel gets fuller and more confusing by the week. On a fall day in October of 2017, Sarah Roberts Miller arranged a meeting for Mom and me with Jean Mummert at her home in Hanceville. The visit with Jean added more details and more pictures to my growing file. Born in 1932, she researched family history most of her adult life, and she also wrote it down. Like my mother and grandmother, she clipped articles from newspapers with family stories. Her information could fill a book about the Johnson descendants.

To put the importance of this visit into perspective, Mother never met or heard of her. Mother told me often about searching for Aunt Bet Price's grave. She remembered the story of her daddy, Albert, and Aunt Bet Price going to Cullman in a wagon to get their sister's children, named Lizzie and Molly. Her story ended there. We now know Jean's dad was Aunt Bet's son. Will we finally place the old pictures from the box with correct people? And, where is the story?

The tangled web of ancestry can bring misery and gloom when information doesn't fit exactly like one thought it would. A problem occurs when too much information comes at one time, and we don't know what to do with it all. An old saying comes back to mind, "I know enough to just be dangerous." At one time, I thought I knew a good bit about my family, but now I think, "I know enough to just be dangerous and possibly incorrect!"

Joel Johnson's ancestors are tangled in webs throughout the United States. Most of the research agrees to the following: Joel married twice. He first married Mary Polly Elliot, and they had nine children. Sarah Susan was born in 1819; William in 1820; Rebecca in 1823; Nancy Polly in 1825; James in 1827; Alfred in 1833; John in 1834; Caleb in 1836; and Joseph Joel, Jr., date unknown. Mary Polly is believed to be buried with her parents. After her death, Joel married Sarah Culwell (Caldwell, Cullwell), and they had eight children. Martha Elizabeth was born in 1843; Lewis Daniel "Coonie" in1844; Levicy in 1845; Presley in 1849; Samuel in 1852; David Taylor in 1853; James Henry in 1859; and Eliza in 1860.

Sarah and Joel rest together in Guinn's Cove. With that said, Joel was a busy family man! His wives were resilient women!

Randall Lewis Price family

Pictures given by Jean from her files of Joel are the best to introduce you to these folks. Needless to say, they were a hardy bunch of people with a robust pioneer spirit. The group picture shows Randall Lewis Price and Martha Elizabeth "Bet" Johnson Price seated in front of a frame unpainted house, like many in the South during those days. Behind them stand their adult children: Sam, Frank (Jean's father), Freeman, Sally, and Mary. Mom told me recently Granny Anna said her she looked like Freeman Price.

In the picture of Eliza, she is standing in front of another frame house with a dusty road behind her. There are no leaves on the tree, so we can assume the first frost came and went. Presley is pictured as an aging fellow with a beard and a hat in his hand. Jean stated Presley married Nancy Henderson and spent his life farming. Was this Presley Johnson buried in a Bangor Cemetery on County Highway 9?

Eliza

Presley

Jim Allen, a classmate and friend of many years, died of cancer in 2017. Growing up, we always knew we were related but never made the connection to Joel Johnson. Now, I know Jim's grandfather was Aunt Bet Price's son. I would love to tell Jim about our shared family. Another discovery from all the research and conversations is classmate and friend, Dianna Johnson Priest, also traced her family back to Joel. Maybe these two friendships were meant to be. What other family waits to be found?

Love, Lice, Romance and Those Johnson Boys

Martha Johnson Grigsby was ninety-three years old when she first told me the story of how to end romance. We trust in the truth of oral history and Mom's memory, as we learn about lice and romance. The story was told: Grandpa James Henry Johnson, as a young unmarried man, looked for a little romance in his life. Henry, as he was called, was born in 1858 and lived until 1930. Boys will be boys in any period of history. Mom said they didn't have any entertainment in those days, so they invented it.

Henry was supposed to be visiting a neighbor fellow who lived nearby. The fellow fathered two daughters Mom called "old maid" sisters. They lived near enough Henry walked for a visit. He started making a daily trip to see these neighbors. He shared his visiting experience with two brothers. They thought he would get tired of the trip and forget about the maids. It didn't happen as quickly as they wanted, so they came up with an idea to end the romancing.

Oliver Johnson

Lice, as you may know, are blood-sucking insects with a place in the history of America. During Henry's time, having body lice was not uncommon, but no one wanted to be known as having them. "It's not a sin to have them, but it's a sin to keep them" was a common thought. Clothes weren't washed often, a bath was sometimes a luxury, and hygiene was not always a priority. The same clothes might be worn for days and days without washing. Lice hang out in clothes and hair on any part of the body.

The brothers weren't concerned about the history of lice. The tale goes, whether for fun or a good reason, they seemed to want the maids out of Henry's life. One of the brothers told Henry, "Henry, look at their heads. They've got lice." We don't know if they made up their story or why these ladies didn't meet the Johnson boys' standards. At this time, the Johnson family had pigs in a pen out back. The plan came together. They told Henry once again the old maids had head lice. He strongly disagreed and went for another visit. While he was away, the brothers got the pig lice. When Henry returned home to rest in a front porch chair, the brothers insisted he be checked for lice. One brother said, "Look what I've found." The other brother, very seriously, "Found another. We told you they had lice." Henry jumped off the porch, pulled off his clothes in the front yard, and looked for lice. That was the last day of visiting the maids.

The Johnson boys were expected to create some excitement for a bit of entertainment if things got boring. The next generation, Henry's sons, were no different. If things got boring, they knew how to create a little fun. On a rainy Saturday night, the corn stood tall in the field. We don't know who, but Joe or Oliver, found a cow bell. Together, they made their way into their dad's field. The bell rang a few times, and they moved to a different location. It was a big field. Their dad thought the old cow from across the river was eating its way from corner to corner of the field. They silenced the bell and moved to a different spot to ring it again, and move and ring. It made for an interesting Saturday night entertainment if you didn't get caught ringing the bell.

Oliver had a sweet side, so my mother says. Albert, another of Henry's boys, visited the big house where Henry lived. Albert decided to leave early and cut through the field to the smaller house below his dad's, where he and Anna lived. It was dark when Anna was ready to leave, so Oliver walked her home. The dark woods and fields were not fitting for a female to walk alone.

I wish I could tell the story the way my mom told it, but I can't put the excitement from her voice into words as she tells the tale. They opened the door to Anna and Albert's house. Inside, there was only an oil lamp for light. A strange man with a coat over his head sat inside the home. The stranger threw the coat over Anna and Oliver as they came in the door. The screaming was heard back at the big house. Mom laughed like she was a little girl as she told her Grandpa's words, "That Albert has gone down there and scared the Hell out of them."

Henry Johnson's family settled in the Moss Bridge area, below Green's Chapel Church. Mom remembered the family stories of the flu pandemic. Joe, Oliver, and sisters, Alder and Sudie died in a period of two weeks from the flu. They are all buried in Green's Chapel Cemetery. Their graves marked with homemade markers.

Mom said I might not want to know all the stories about those Johnson boys of Moss Bridge. She reminded me if things got boring, they created their own entertainment.

Frances Darnell Whited

Frances McGuire Johnson, a Strong Woman

Frances McGuire Johnson

The picture of Frances McGuire Johnson stayed in my folder of ideas for a long time. It was another rainy, gloomy dark day when I picked up her picture one more time. I searched for the right words, maybe something respectful to say. There had to be some words for this strong looking woman from my past. She was born around 1856 and died on April 2, 1936, the daughter of William J. and Elizabeth "Betsy" (Cornelius) McGuire. Museum records indicate her grandparents were Moses Cornelius, born in South Carolina in 1784, and Cynthia Bynum Cornelius, born in 1791. The family of William J. McGuire could not be found. Family stories told William's family was from Ireland, but I haven't found documentation. Moses Cornelius and the Cornelius family are well documented in Blount County. From *The Heritage of Blount County, Alabama, Volume 5,* p. 84, I read Moses and Cynthia were in Alabama by the year 1819. In 1819, Moses purchased the first grist mill in the area built in 1818. The mill was located about four miles southwest of the town of Oneonta.

Frances McGuire became the wife of James Henry Johnson. She gave birth to a long list of children, probably in her own bed, with nothing for the pain of childbirth. Her grave is marked with a concrete, homemade stone, in Green's Chapel Cemetery. Though I never knew her, I helped put flowers on her grave every First Sunday in May all of my life. When I look at her features in the old photograph, I see reflections of my Grandpa Albert's face. What can one picture tell us about a long ago relative? Somehow, I wanted to tie her to the dusty roads of my past, if only through her son, Albert.

Frances's facial features are reflected in pictures of my Grandpa Albert. With her hair pulled back, we see her wide nose and high cheekbones: Her full face stands out. Positioned by the wooden fence, I notice the dress she is wearing for the picture is too large and has the sleeves rolled up. She is wearing an apron to protect this dress from the daily, wifely chores.

In the Johnson family folder, I found another picture of three men. Mother told me they were her Grandpa's brothers. I placed the known Johnson pictures side by side, and they began to tell a story of their time in history. When I look at the brothers, I suppose they are Frances's brothers-in-law, dressed in their Sunday best. They would not have worked in the fields in these clothes. Remembering the phrase, "A picture is worth a thousand words," I think these pictures could be worth a thousand words. I focused on the brother in the

David Taylor ? (in the center) and Brothers in Their Sunday Best

middle, who looked the most like my Grandpa Albert. Mom said his name was Dav. Could this be David Taylor Johnson, born in 1853? His suit is very wrinkled, and the jacket sleeves are too short. The pants are obviously too large in the waist and hips, and the legs too long, puddling up around his ankles. The brother to his left has a long jacket, maybe a bit longer than it should be, and his pants fit a little better, but his shirt collar appears oversized. The brother to his right seems to have tightened his pants with the belt. As I analyze these old photos, I feel a bit of gloom come over me for even trying to dissect their lives with only pictures. Concentrating on their clothing is an injustice to their stories and directs attention away from the people.

Mother's story of the flu came back to me, as she told it year after year when we decorated their graves. She probably heard it over and over in her childhood because of its outstanding memory in her mind. James Henry, her grandpa, never got the flu. Mother said it was because he drank alcohol every day. Frances became too sick to help him care for the others and was carried by buggy to a neighbor's house. Frances and James Henry survived the flu, only to bury four of their children in a period of two weeks. The handsome son, Oliver, battled his way to what everyone believed to be recovery. Mom tells he said he needed fresh air, and they raised a window near his bed. He died from pneumonia. Mom said relatives blamed Oliver's death on too much fresh air. ("The estimated global mortality from the 1918-1920 pandemic was anywhere between 30 and 50 million," quote from *www.flu.gov.pandemic/history1918*)

The picture of the Johnson brothers remains a favorite family picture. We don't know where the picture is taken. The clothes of these brothers speak the word "hand-me-downs." Good clothes were handed down to others who needed them or wanted to wear them. There was no shame attached. It was the economical thing to do. These handed-down items started a new life and journey in someone else's story. I am reminded of the writings of Alabama educator and writer, Wayne Flynt. His books told us about Alabama's poor whites, their pride, and Southern culture.

The strong woman from my picture lived on, enduring the loss of her children, and heard of neighbors who died in the pandemic. Did she have the strength to stand by the grave sites as they buried them one by one? Frances talked to the family about her folks coming from Ireland. She knew about the Great War, World War I, and heard news of families who lost loved ones in faraway places. I read a beautiful quote once but can't give credit to an author. All I wrote down were the words: From an Irish headstone, "Death leaves a heartache no one can heal, love leaves a memory no one can steal." Maybe, I saved this quote for Frances McGuire Johnson, the strong Johnson woman who said her family came from Ireland.

A Revolutionary War Relative

The love of local history and ancestors carry an individual down many old roads. Growing up, any road leaving Cleveland carried me to family. It seemed to me we were related to everyone in Blount County. At the time, I wasn't interested in who fought in World War II, World War I, the Civil War, the Indian War, the Revolutionary War, or any war for that matter. I heard the stories and saw a lot of tombstones, but I didn't take time to learn about these people.

As the stories for this book developed, I started finding more and more relatives were part of the great wars of our country. I asked myself why I neglected this part of my history. The answer may be my hatred for war. I saw the effects that World War II, the Korean War, and the Vietnam War had on people I knew. Another answer was my fear of guns and the misuse of weapons. With the reading, researching, and writing about family, I began looking at the history of my relatives who served in these wars as something very important.

When I found Sampson McCarty fought in the Indian War, I showed the government stamped card to Amy Rhudy at the Blount County Memorial Museum. I strongly dislike the period of history which included the Indian Removal. I saw it as cruel and inhuman treatment of the people who owned these lands before the coming of the "white man." Amy was pleased to see the stamped "Indian War" on the document, and we made a copy for the museum files. This small bit of family history renewed my interest in the military history of my family. I put aside my personal prejudice, fears, and negative thoughts about war and started searching for the relatives who fought, not judging their reasons or ideas.

My copy of ***The Heritage of Blount County, Alabama, Vol. 5,*** is a well used, marked up, very loved book. It's always nearby. So many people did the hard work and research for the history of Blount County. The book helped as I created my family tree on a chart with branches going in all directions. With it and many other sources, my tree's branches began to fill. Happy with my chart, I rolled it out across my dining room table as I checked relationships and dates for my stories. Somewhere on my tree was my Revolutionary War connection. A goal to find a relative from the Revolutionary War became a focus for my reading.

While waiting for the folks to edit my stories, I put all the writing away. I became restless with the two last stories about Tuscaloosa Road. I waited on documentation for the old road again. At night, I started rereading *The Heritage of Blount County*. This time I would just read, and hopefully, something overlooked showed up.

Mother never talked about any Cornelius relatives, but I found them, lost in time, related to my Grandpa Albert Johnson. His grandmother was Elizabeth M. "Betsy" Cornelius. This information went on the tree, and I attended the "Four Families of Blount County" reunion and confirmed my research. I didn't do anything with data but add dates and the names of descendants of Moses and Cynthia Bynum Cornelius and descendants of William Cornelius and Lettice Martha Cargile. My tree continued to branch out deeper into the faraway past.

William Cornelius, Revolutionary Soldier

One night, I read again about Moses Cornelius and added the information to the Johnson family story. Much later, I realized I became too focused on the details of creating a story and missed valuable information to help find my Revolutionary War relative. For some reason, Moses didn't leave me in peace. Did he have more to say? It was a brutal nineteen degrees outside as I sat with my coffee and my favorite book, *The Heritage of Blount County*. Miss Molly dog and I would not go out today. I told her to go back to bed, and I read about Moses.

With a cold wind blowing outside, on page 156, I found my Revolutionary War ancestor. "William Cornelius (1754-1842) was a soldier of the Revolutionary War. He served as a Pvt. with the North Carolina Field Artillery, and was mustered out at a camp near York, Pa., May, 1788. In 1832 he received 640 acres of Bounty land in Tennessee." William married Lettice Cargile in 1774, and they had eleven children. One of them was Moses. William and his family came to Blount County, Alabama, in early the 1800s. He settled near the land where I worked for twenty-five years, the now Oneonta City School. During those twenty-five years, I never knew my great-great-great-grandfather was buried in the old Cornelius Cemetery above the school. My son, Bart Rainey, William's great-great-great-great-grandson, graduated from Oneonta High School in 1988. The strong Johnson woman, Frances E. McGuire Johnson, whose picture I studied many times, was William's great grand-daughter.

With a smile, I think, perhaps the spirit of that Revolutionary War soldier watched over his descendants as they passed through the school doors each day. Maybe, his Revolutionary War spirit gave Frances the courage to face the flu pandemic that took her children.

Frances Darnell Whited

Mad Dogs and Moss Bridge

As a child, my mother called out to me, "Don't pet that stray dog!" I never knew why she was so upset about a dog walking down the road in front of our house. Now, years later when I take my morning walk with my three old girl dogs, who had been strays, a story came back to me. I needed to hear my mom's story again from her.

No wonder she had such a passion to protect us from stray dogs. When I sat down to talk with her about her "mad dog" story, the subject was still vivid in her ninety-four year old mind. First of all, the way to pronounce the words mad dog is "maddog." It sounds more like "madog." Mother's dialect and passion for this story cannot really be written down with her enthusiasm, but I'll try.

Mother was born in 1923 and grew up hearing stories from her family about dogs who had "gone mad." To a young child, the symptoms of a dog with rabies as told by the adults in the family were terrible. Even worse, the story of a human with rabies left a child afraid to get off the front porch. As a youngster, she lived near Moss Bridge in a small house near her grandfather's big house in Blount County. There was a river and corn patch near the big house where her grandparents lived. The milk was kept in a flowing spring of fresh water to keep it cold. Mom walked by herself to the river or the spring to get whatever her mother or grandmother stored there. Walking along, her imagination filled with 'mad dogs' coming out of the field and woods. She said, "I would never have sent my children off by themselves to get that milk!"

She remembered the family dog named Nero, who had not gotten the rabies vaccination. Being bitten by a stray dog, "Poor old Nero went mad. First, he couldn't drink water, and they had to kill him." This is a really bad childhood memory for my mom!

Louis Pasteur is credited with developing the first rabies vaccine. Rabies was a serious threat across France during his time. It was years before laws required animals in the United Stated to be vaccinated and the threat of "madogs" to go away.

Mom remembered Jesse Horton, a neighbor on Tuscaloosa Road. He was also a cousin, and his sister, Omie, the housekeeper for W.B. Roberts. Mr. Jesse worked in the field with his birddog beside him. His dog was vaccinated, but Jesse saw a stray dog coming into the field. The dog never had a chance. Mr. Jesse hit it with his hoe and buried it deep in the field. I suppose it was better to take action than take the risk of a sick dog. Mom said Mr. Jesse's words of wisdom about stray dogs were, "If you don't have something to kill it with, stand still, and let it go by."

Moss Bridge

We still have stray dogs, unloved and unwanted, who ramble up. My son and I gave many strays a new home with little thought of the dreaded rabies. We simply load them up for a trip to our friends at the Animal Hospital and get a rabies shot.

A Blount Countian took this photograph of Old Moss Bridge on the day before the bridge was torn down. The trestles may be seen in a distant pasture.

On a Saturday evening, I took my mom for a drive down the Moss Bridge Road. Cotton fields came into view, and there was a fine house near the river. Mom told me one more time about living in the small house near Moss Bridge and her fear of going to the river alone. Somewhere up the river, she walked as a little girl. We drove across the new bridge and found our way back to Green's Chapel and didn't encounter any stray dogs.

Frances Darnell Whited

Possum in a Pot

Our modern grocery stores are amazing things. We stroll down the aisles with a grocery cart and find foods our ancestors may never have seen. Colorful, fresh vegetables are there to welcome us year round. If we desire meat for the daily meal, it's there, in a package, ready to cook.

When my Granddaddy Johnson was growing up in Blount County, he probably never saw the luxuries of grocery stores. His large family grew their vegetables and canned what they needed for the winter months. Meat, for the family table, was hunted in the forests or grown at home. A funny story told by my mother was about a possum meant to scare the Johnson family. The possum was placed in the mailbox by persons unknown. It waited for someone to come for mail.

Possums are common critters that roam the country at night. I've never thought they were pretty to look at, and they make a hissing sound if trapped. They are not really dangerous when you leave them alone. If you live on a farm, a possum can steal your chickens, turkeys, or ducks. We've learned in recent years possums carry diseases which can be passed to humans and pets. They may also be infested with fleas, ticks, mites, and lice. Possums are hosts for cat and dog fleas, especially in urban environments. With that said, I would never think of eating a possum. During the Great Depression and other hard times, possum hunts were not uncommon. A good dog and a good gun were about all you needed to hunt. I read possum hunting was not a rich man's sport; instead it was a sport for poor folks who needed food.

Clint Johnson

Back to Mom's story, it related the morning the Johnson boys found a possum in the mailbox. Someone stuffed the old critter in the box during the night. It was meant for a joke to scare the person who opened the mailbox. Mom couldn't remember who found the possum in the post that day. They closed it back up in the box and told their mother what they found. A possum found was not to be wasted in those good old days. The morning joke turned into a family meal after it was successfully processed. Possum dumplings were not an uncommon meal in those times.

I decided to do a little reading about this meal and found a website, *HillbillyCrockpot.com*. I'm not going to be cooking possum, but it made for an interesting read. If you find a possum in your mailbox, and you have fallen on hard times, just clean the critter and remove the insides, find a pot with a good tight lid, and cook it until the meat comes off the bone. You will need the following:

8 Big Taters	pepper to taste and whatever other spices you like
2 big spoons of butter	1 cooking pot with a good tight lid
1 big spoon of sugar	
a pinch or two of salt	Cook the possum in a pot, and dinner's ready.

As for me, I'll push my grocery cart along as I stroll down the aisles. I haven't noticed any possum in the meat section lately!

Frances Darnell Whited

The Boat that Sailed Away

The story goes World War I and the draft were taking all the young men of Blount County. Laney was Grandpa Albert's brother. His draft card showed he was born on April 5, 1876, and registered on June 5, 1917. He signed his registration with an "X". Well, that's not much of a story. There must be a story hiding somewhere. On my visit to Jeanette Sherrer's house, she and Mom talked about her neighbors. Ah, a story was coming. I knew. As I must have done as a child, I sat quietly, waited, and listened as these ladies talked. I learned where Laney's children, Glen and Robbie Jean, lived. I drifted away looking at family pictures around the walls of Jean's home when it happened. The story began.

"Did I ever tell you about…?" is a phrase my mom uses a lot when she is recalling another tale.

**Laney Johnson, Glen's Dad
Albert's Brother**

"Did I ever tell you about Uncle Laney and the War? He was supposed to leave with the Army. Him and another man, I believe, it was a Grigsby, got drafted. They had to go away and were waiting in a long line to sign in to leave on a boat. Laney whispered to the fellow, 'When they get busy, we'll just start walking away. I'm not dying in any trenches.' And walk away, he did. The boat sailed away without that Johnson boy.

I don't know about the other man, but Grandma hid Laney in a corn box in the barn. She carried food to him like she was going to feed the pigs. Several times, the law came looking for him. One time, one of them even sat down on the corn box. Grandma lived around Moss Bridge, which was a covered bridge back then. They didn't have many visitors. They never found him." Now, that's oral history, pure and simple!

This story came to me again from another source, Jean Mummert, a long-time Johnson story collector. I learned about her from Sarah Roberts Miller. Jean's wealth of Johnson information was first shared with me in a letter passed on to Sarah and mailed to me. The names of Joel Johnson's two wives and their children were listed, along with the names of the folks they married. On a day too hot to go outside, I phoned Jean to thank her for the information. My conversation turned to stories about the Johnsons I heard from my mother. Ah, when I get the same story from a different source, the work is all worth it! I asked if she knew or heard any stories about Laney Johnson. And, this is the answer: "My grandmother wanted to go visit Henry (Laney's Daddy) for a week. She was told in no uncertain terms she could visit if she asked no questions and talked about nothing she saw. She visited for a week. Three times a day someone carried food to the animals, and they weren't gone long. No one talked about it. She never fed the animals." Years later, she learned the family hid Laney during the war. Did they save his life? Maybe.

The War ended in 1918. He escaped the war, the trenches, and any punishment. Uncle Laney died in 1974 and is buried in Green's Chapel Cemetery along with all those other Johnson boys from Moss Bridge.

Frances Darnell Whited

Uncle Ace: On Johnson Road

Imogene, Martha Frances and Inez

If you drive south down Highway 79 from Cleveland, when you see Green's Chapel Cemetery on your right, you will also see the remains of Gilliland Store on your left. The name of the county road to the left is Johnson Road. Drive slowly, and Ace Johnson's homeplace remains on the right. When I carry Mom for a drive, sometimes, we take that road so she can see the old house. As a girl, she rode her bicycle down Old Tuscaloosa Road to visit these cousins. She always sighs, and says, "I had some good times at this place."

Uncle Ace enjoyed a daily trip to Oneonta. Locals said, "You couldn't go to Oneonta without meeting Ace Johnson, either coming or going." Jeanette Sherrer told about when she was a child. Uncle Ace offered a nickel to get a hundred gray hairs from his graying head. She laughed and said he counted to make sure there were one hundred. Mother had no pictures of Uncle Ace or his wife, Luvina. I looked many times in the picture boxes and could not understand why that happened. Mom was very close with the girl cousins and visited often. Ace and Luvina had a large family: Orban, Ray, Walton, Louise, Inez, Annie Ruth, Imogene, John, Margie, Argie, and Vera Mae. Why were there no pictures? There must be a reason. If I couldn't find a picture, I still wanted a story about the family.

Janet Gilliland Ray became my source. Her mother, Louise, was a daughter of Uncle Ace. In the past, if you lived in Cleveland, you knew about Lester and Louise Johnson Gilliland's grocery store and garage. Janet and I began to talk by phone, and I realized how much family information she had. She told me there were so many children; they probably didn't have money for pictures. Janet's memories added to my story about Ace Johnson and his family.

It was around nineteen degrees outside this morning; Miss Molly dog was asleep in her bed. I settled in to make phone calls, and Janet was first on my list. Our conversation led me to the following story as written to me in an e-mail. Her first story brings honor and sadness. It begins: "Walton and Orban served in the Army during World War II, 1939-1945. Uncle Ray went to join and was sent home and advised to see a doctor. After his visit, he was told the spot on his lip was cancer. Back then, there weren't facilities to help treat him. My mom, Louise, was his caregiver.

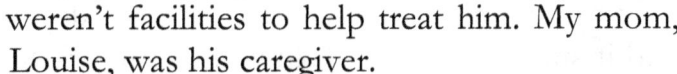

The cancer spread through his jaw bone, and Mom wrapped gauze around his head to keep the bone in place. She said Uncle Ray never complained.

Ray Johnson died on October 4, 1944."

Janet lived a brief walk from her Granddaddy Ace. One of her favorite memories was the time spent sitting on the side porch. The fun story has an Old South charm! "Big Momma (Luvina) and Papa (Ace) had three porches around the house. One on the front, side, and back, and we loved to sit on the side porch at night and tell stories and catch up on things. I think it's called gossip. With no telephone or television (well, we did have a radio), we enjoyed the porches at night, listening to the crickets, and catching lightning bugs. Oh! And, I loved all the ghost stories they told. Several times my uncles who worked the three to eleven shift told us they saw something floating around in the Green's Chapel Cemetery when they came in from Birmingham. I really don't know if the stories were true or not, but to this day, I will not go in the cemetery by myself. I would die of a heart attack if I saw a ghost floating around the graves."

Janet's memories told about the cows her Big Mama and Papa had. "They always had milk, buttermilk, and butter (which Big Mama made by taking the cream off the top of the milk). I took the milk to the spring below the chicken house to keep it cool. (No refrigerator) They had chickens, so they had eggs and fried chicken. One day, Big Mama decided it was time for me to learn the procedure to fry chicken. This meant learning to ring the chicken's neck, boiling water to pluck the chicken, cutting up the chicken, and then, frying the chicken. Now first of all, I am NOT A CHICKEN KILLER!! I told her I didn't think I could do it. But, nothing I said changed her mind. So, she told me to catch the chicken by the neck and swing it around a couple of times. As you can guess, by being a first timer, my swinging around didn't do the job. I released the chicken, and it started running. (Can you blame it?) Next, Big Mama told me to go and catch it again, and she would finish the job. Well, I tried to tell her and believe me, she never asked me again. To this day, I have never killed a chicken."

Smokey, Janet's Welch pony, was kept in Uncle Ace's barn, so she had good reason to spend weekends with them. On Saturday morning, she would peep in the kitchen to see Big Mama humming and making her homemade biscuits. Uncle Ace, with a smile on his face, was up and ready to share breakfast. Janet thinks Big Mama's humming was the ingredient that made her biscuits so good. Janet never told the other grandchildren her Papa bought her the prettiest black boots to wear as she rode her pony. He couldn't afford to buy them all boots.

Gilliland's Store Today (2018)

Janet's memories are so much like my memories with my Johnson grandparents. We were loved and knew it. Again, I treasure the oral history which can be shared. What a wonderful family we had! We built amazing memories.

Janet's words carried me back to breakfast on Tuscaloosa Road with my Grandpa Albert. Janet said it all, "Oh, how l loved those days!

Ocean Sounds from the Past

My Grandpa Albert never got to see the Pacific Ocean, but on the mantle of his living room fireplace sat two large seashells. They were a treasure placed out of the way of curious little hands. We were told you could hear the ocean if you placed the shell to your ear. My brother and I were fascinated with the idea of hearing the ocean's sound when we were allowed to hold the shells. Time passed, and I forgot about the old shells from my grandparents' home. One day, my mom phoned and told me she had a gift for my son. The gift, she said, was over a hundred years old. I couldn't imagine what it was, and she wouldn't tell me. This is how the ocean came to Blount County long ago.

Jerry and Darnell

Grandpa Albert's cousin, Lizzie Fisher, had a sister who moved to California. The story goes she visited the sister and came home with seashells. They were dirty, smelly, and in need of cleaning when given as gifts to Anna and Albert. The cousin told them the story of listening to the sound of the ocean with these beautiful shells. They cleaned the shells. At that point, they started their lives on Grandpa's fireplace mantle. My grandparents shared the story with their children: Martha, Charles, and Bud. They explained it to visitors in their home on Tuscaloosa Road. Many years later, they told the story to their grandchildren, Darnell and Jerry. Carefully, everyone listened for the ocean, put the shell to the ear, and there was the magnificent sound of the Pacific Ocean. The two shells became family treasures and listening to the ocean was a shared gift. The shells were not toys to play with because they could be broken. We held them tenderly and placed them over the ear. When it was time to listen, the only talking came from the instructor, "Don't drop them." Jerry and I stood quietly, very still, when we held the shells. It was a wonderful thing! There, in the shell, was the sound of the Pacific Ocean with its waves lapping the beach. How could this be? The hum of faraway waves captured in the spiral conch shell for us to hear in Alabama.

Mother's gift that day was the two treasured shells from her childhood. It would truly ruin the story if I explained about the scientist's theory of the sound in the shells. It would also break my mother's heart to know the ocean sounds of her past were not real. That day, she told me she placed the shells to her ears to hear the sound, but could no longer hear the waves, even with her hearing aids. She asked if the sounds were still there. I placed the shells, one by one to my ears, as I did as a little girl in my grandpa's house. I smiled and told her the sound was still there. That was the perfect answer. The sound is still there to be passed on to loved ones.

Sometimes, it's better to put aside your scientific knowledge, and enjoy the myths and stories of long ago. My son allowed me to keep the shells, and they rest peacefully on top of the China cabinet which stores other treasures from my past. I look at the shells and think of the people who held them carefully to their ears and listened to the sound of the ocean. One day, when I can no longer hear the ocean, I will gently hand the shells to my son for safe keeping.

Albert Johnson, the Gentle Trapper

Albert Johnson was a trapper in the winter months and the "ice man" in the hot Alabama summers of the 1940's and 1950's in Blount County. His and his wife, Anna's, white frame house sat back off the dirt road. He parked the old Chevrolet truck used to make his deliveries of ice or hides under the catalpa tree in the evenings, except when the caterpillars came. He also farmed the land around his house. He prayed on his knees in the big barn behind his house on the Tuscaloosa Road in Cleveland, Alabama. They raised three children together: Martha Frances, Bud, and Charles. When his day was over and his treasured truck parked safely under the tree, weather permitting, he sat on the front porch watching travelers pass.

Albert Johnson and Darnell

Behind his house, within close walking distance to the back porch, were a series of connected buildings. These buildings held fascinating spots with strange tools which needed to be investigated by a young granddaughter. The one closest to the house was the "Well House." We, in the family, called it that for a simple reason. The well for drawing water was located there. A long, skinny bucket hung ready for use. It was attached to the biggest rope these eyes had ever seen. The rope was never carelessly dropped into the well. It circled around a pulley setup and was firmly secured to a wooden cylinder with a handle for lowering the bucket into the well.

Besides the well, this building accommodated a low concrete creation of Grandpa's design, a hand-built, "ice chest." It ran the length of the wall. How many blocks of ice could it hold? I don't remember. The modern method of refrigeration had not made it into Grandpa's house. In the summer months, ice was stored in the concrete box. The huge blocks of ice were cracked and chipped with an ice pick for family use and for sweet iced tea.

When summer left, Grandpa used the well house walls to help with his winter job. In the winter months, animal skins, stretched over boards, hung around the walls to dry. Because of my acceptance and love for this silver haired man, in my early years, I never thought of the animal skins on the walls as ever having life. By Grandpa's magic, pelts were created. This gentle man could never be cruel to animals or cause pain to a mink, raccoon, muskrat, or fox. To him, the animals of the forest and those that became pelts were not the same animals. Back in the day, a possum hide was worth a whole dollar. Mink was a treasure. At this time, there were no laws or shame involved in trapping. It was a poor man's way of making extra money. As children, we never saw how the animal became a pelt.

Though the furs were tempting to reach and touch, my brother and I learned early in life not to go in this building without permission. To be caught in there was sure to bring a harsh look from Grandpa's blue eyes. One of his most severe by-words, "Consarn," was directed at us. For those who are not schooled in the art of swearing, without swearing, this is a brief lesson. My Grandpa's word, "Consarn," is found in early eighteenth century British literature. A good Christian family man never used the word, "Damn." There were many interesting words said instead of using a real curse word!

After Grandpa's verbal discipline, several swift switches from Mom's hickory were guaranteed to come next. Her hickories were the thinnest limb a hedge bush offered. It never broke when used on a young behind or the calf of bare legs. A friend was quoted as saying, "The worst was when we had to pick our own! It was a lose-lose situation!"

Next to the Well House was the "Wood Shed." Grandpa stored wood for the wood burning kitchen stove and double fireplaces. The traps used hung on the walls of this shed. The next building down stored the canned food which had been "put up" during canning season.

Temptation feeds the spirit and weakens the will of both young and old alike, so my brother and I found ways to slip into the buildings without being caught. We touched the furs, and sometimes, we stood and stared at the traps on the back walls of these forbidden buildings. Viewed by my young eyes, traps were a necessary, but sinister, part of my grandpa's world. There was an assortment on the wall with the most fearful looking ones placed near the ceiling. There were traps of all sizes. Some looked like wooden boxes, and other traps had jaws of steel. The steel traps looked like monsters with terrible teeth when my brother and I dared to make up pretend stories about Grandpa's traps. The tales Mom told, well, we almost expected them to jump of the walls and snap off the hands and toes of snooping children.

It seemed strange and unlikely to find birdseed kept in the Well House. The seed was for the birds Grandpa loved to feed and watch. He allowed no cats around his house. Cats: the natural enemies of his bird friends. Bluebirds, robins, and cardinals were his favorites. He knew what each liked to eat and how to encourage nesting places for the birds he attracted.

As soon as weather turned the evenings warm, Mom let my brother and me walk the half-mile down the Old Tuscaloosa Road to visit our Johnson grandparents. Grandpa, in his overalls, rocked in his rocker on the front porch. On one particular day, we found him sitting on the steps waiting for us. His eyes seemed to brighten when he saw us coming, and he motioned for us to follow him. Following and trying to match his light, brisk, steps was not easy. We bounced along behind him to the backyard and on to the Well House, the strange place we were forbidden to go into without permission. He paused a few steps from the building and said he had a surprise for us. Grandpa never had money for surprises. This had to be special!

We waited outside while he went inside. He moved the grapevine that grew too close to the entrance and disappeared inside the dark building. We heard him moving around inside. We both must have listened hard for some clue to tell us about the surprise. When he came out, Grandpa held one of his box traps with both hands. He carefully carried it to the steps of the back porch. As he walked, he told us the surprise.

Grandpa caught a live, male cardinal in his box trap. It probably walked into the box and pecked the trigger that held the box open. This unusual catch was ours to carry home and free. Grandpa eased the box open and reached in for the bird. It was so red. The bird made one frantic flutter, a cry of sorts, and then, it appeared to become calm.

The bird Grandpa's hand brought out of the box was the most beautiful cardinal I had ever seen. He had the reddest of red feathers. The red bird died as my grandpa reached to touch him. Without speaking to either of us, he gently placed the bird back in the cage. His shoulders appeared to slump, and his walk was not as light as we went back to the front porch without the surprise.

My brother and I spoke on our walk back home that evening, but we never talked about the beautiful red bird again. Grandpa continued to trap until old age hindered his walking, and Alabama laws changed. At his death, his traps sold to strangers. And his granddaughter? She grew up to believe all of God's creatures should be allowed to live in peace, free from guns, cages, traps, and free from neglect and abuse.

Teacakes in Granny Anna's Kitchen

Someone asked me why I put a sugar cookie recipe in the middle of my stories. It seemed the natural place for this valued recipe. I grew up waiting for the welcome smell of fresh baked teacakes to greet me when I visited my grandparents. It took me years of baking cookies to find the recipe of my memories. Granny Anna and her sister, Myrtle, who lived in Five Points, both baked what they called teacakes. I heard from my classmate, Jerry Cornelius, who lived near my Aunt Myrtle, the smell and taste of teacakes was something really special. We talked about these special cookies and decided they learned this wonderful recipe from their mother. With that said, Anna's stories must include a teacake recipe.

Anna May Roberts was born on May 12, 1895. She married Albert Johnson on December 17, 1911. When I knew her, she spent a lot of time in her bed at their home on the Tuscaloosa Road in Cleveland. Unlike my grandpa, she didn't talk to me very much. I know a lot about her from old photographs kept in family picture boxes.

Their home was simple. I remember only the bare necessarys. I walked from room to room in the house of my memories, and I entered the living room where she had a bed near the fireplace. There were usually only three chairs in the room. Grandpa dipped snuff, a smokeless tobacco made from ground tobacco leaves. His chair was near his spit pot, but there were stains on the concrete in front of the fireplace. He missed his target more than one time. Each of the two bedrooms included a bed, a chair, and a bureau for clothes and quilts. Everything was handed down, worn with age. There was no indoors bathroom. In the winter months, the only heat came from the double fireplaces and the wood burning stove in the kitchen. Granny's kitchen had a pie safe, a flour bin, an old table with a few chairs, and the wood stove. There was no running water in the house, but there was a small stand by the back door for the water bucket and dipper. On her good days, Granny got out of bed and cooked, and she was best remembered for those cooking skills. She could make amazing chicken and dumplings for Sunday after church.

Annie Ruth Holt, Anna and Martha Frances

The taste and smell of those dumplings! Amazing. Breakfast was usually homemade biscuits with whatever was available. One of my favorite breakfast meals included what Grandpa called "red eye" gravy. It was made with sausage grease and a bit of coffee that caused the red eye. We spooned it over warm biscuits and enjoyed every crumb. When strawberries were in season, Grandpa picked the juicy red berries, smashed them up, and we spooned those over warm biscuits. Granny never used a recipe for anything she cooked. She simply cooked from memory.

Many years after Granny's death, I asked Mom about the recipe for Granny's teacakes. She watched her mother make them. Granny watched her mother… measure, mix, roll, cut into circles, and bake. Unfortunately, Mom never learned Granny's recipe. Granny made them with ease in the same bowl she made biscuits and dumplings. No flour was ever wasted. When we walked in the little house, we instantly knew if she baked teacakes. The smell filled the air, and we knew where to find these luxuries. They were a light, golden brown and so moist. They waited for two little kids, my brother and me, in the kitchen.

Without the handed down recipe, I spent years searching for the taste from my childhood. By accident, I found a recipe which was so close to Granny's teacake recipe in an old *Betty Crocker's New Picture Cook Book*. (I could not find the copyright date.) On page 199, a recipe called Ethel's Sugar Cookies had simple ingredients which might have been in

Granny's kitchen. Many years passed as I experimented with the recipe. I finally found a near match for those wonderful teacakes.

No story about Anna's kitchen is complete without telling one more story about a cough cure. My brother and I didn't have a cough, but we knew about the cough medicine in the kitchen. A teaspoon from this bottle tucked in the pie safe cured a cough. We were not supposed to bother the cough syrup, but kids are curious about the things they are not supposed to touch. We took our first sip one cold evening when all the adults were talking around the fireplace in the living room. Did we get a bit tipsy? Well, with a sip, we only felt warm and happy. We might have gotten away with our tasting if we stopped with the first sip. But, we tried it on another visit, and maybe, one more time. It is accurate to say we liked the taste and the feeling from a sip of cough medicine. One day, Grandpa realized the cough medicine was slowly disappearing. He had not had a cough. How did he know it was my brother and me? I don't remember. I

Darnell's Version of Granny's Cookies

don't remember the punishment or the name of the whiskey, but I remember the bottle was moved out of sight and reach.

During the holiday season, I bake teacakes for my family and think of Granny's simple recipe and the warmth of her kitchen. My revised recipe is copied for you to share with your family and create memories for their future. Don't leave the kitchen, or they will burn. Stay and enjoy the smell as they slowly turn that golden brown. And, if I get a cough around the time the days turn cold, I remember my little brother and the medicine we found tucked away in the pie safe.

Recently, I read Dennis Martin's book, *Grandpa' Porch Swing Stories.* I knew Dennis for years, as pastor of Westside Baptist Church in Cleveland where my parents were charter members. When I read Dennis's words about his grandma's Sunday dinners, I knew we shared a common bond. His delightful description of a wood burning stove was so detailed. I was transported back to my Granny's kitchen and the smell of teacakes. Dennis's grandma also baked this wonderful cookie. On page seven, his words said it all, "There ain't nothing better than teacakes and a big glass of cold milk from the ice box." I couldn't say it better.

Anna's Postcard

When I found the postcard addressed to Miss Anna Roberts, I became so excited. This held more personal information about my grandmother than I knew. Not to insult my granny, but most of my memories of her are Granny reclining in her bed. I came to believe she took to her bed when she didn't want to deal with day-to-day developments and waited out the drama of life. She enjoyed her pillows and quilts, and the years passed.

Anna Roberts married Albert Johnson in December of 1911. With magnifying glass in hand, I could read the postmark on the card as 1911 and read the following:

> "Hello How are you. I am all ok don't ans until you Hear
> from me got your letter to day
> Barns"

In Granny Anna's picture box were other postcards addressed to Miss Anna Roberts. There were pictures of other young men. Who WAS the man in the car? But most of all, who WAS the man writing the postcard? Mother always said, "Those Roberts girls had lots of boyfriends." There must have been a life for Anna before she took to her bed. She was only a teenager when she married Albert. Maybe, there was disappointment and heartbreak. Could one of the men in the picture be a boyfriend who moved away? Was Barns the man before my grandpa? The name of the Hotel is torn off, removing a clue. Was she writing to someone just before she wed Grandpa in December? When I showed Mom the cards, she didn't recognize anyone and didn't know about Barns. Barns continues to stoke my imagination, and the story ends with the mystery of the 1911 postcard.

Anna's Post Card from Barns

Another mystery

Sassafras Tea, Rabbit Tobacco, and Me

Anna Roberts Johnson believed in the healing powers of native plants. Like many others of her time, she learned from her parents which plants could be used for all sorts of ailments. Sassafras and rabbit tobacco were her two favorite medicinal plants. Anna used the root bark of sassafras to make tea. She sometimes sipped it in bed.

Albert and Anna (Roberts) Johnson

No one remembered why Anna first "took to her bed." Mom seemed to think she had a heart condition. As for me, I think it may have been overuse of sassafras tea, too many smokes of rabbit tobacco, or maybe, the boyfriend who got away.

In her later years, all the family said Grandpa Albert waited on her, "hand and foot." I always understood "hand and foot" meant he did everything for her. I don't know why he stopped looking for her sassafras and rabbit tobacco, but he did. Maybe, he just got old. After Grandpa's death, she moved in with our family. Granny Anna sent me to look for what she wanted. I grew up knowing what sassafras leaves and rabbit tobacco looked like. I must confess: I never drank the tea. I tried to smoke rabbit tobacco once. I became so sick for years to come the smell of the leaves was unbearable.

In a very old china cabinet from New Orleans, I keep things given to me from my mom's house on Tuscaloosa Road. One of my most treasured items is my Granny Anna's corn cob pipes. Mom kept them safe for years, and then, passed them onto me. One is made from a corn cob and a hollow reed. I questioned whether it was homemade, and Mom said Grandpa made it. It was always Granny's favorite and used the most.

Frances Darnell Whited

There was a place on the river near Swann Bridge where Grandpa knew the reeds grew. Corncobs were plentiful, so after the crops were in and fall came, he made her pipes. In later years, my Uncle Bud got her a manufactured pipe. According Mom, Granny Anna said it wasn't as good as a homemade pipe.

Recently, I started reading about both plants and corncob pipes. There is so much to learn. I found corncob pipes are back in demand. I journeyed on to reading about sassafras. It was speculated to cure about everything to ail a human. It was used for urinary tract disorders, swelling in the nose and throat, syphilis, bronchitis, high blood pressure, gout, arthritis, skin problems, cancer, as a tonic, blood purifier, sprains, and insect bites or stings. I may have left out something! Good ole' Rabbit Tobacco, sometimes called Life Everlasting, was used for colds, asthma, congestion of the sinuses, and stomach and intestinal disorders. There wasn't much illness these two plants couldn't improve.

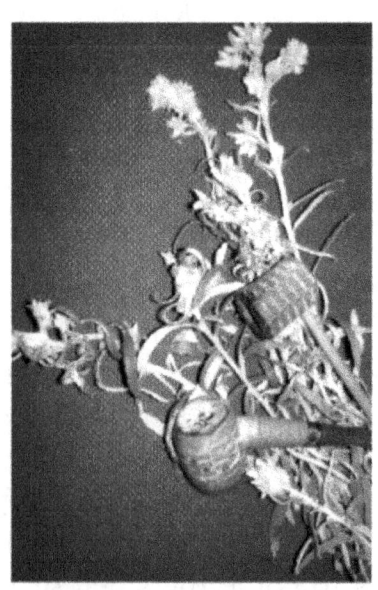

Rabbit Tobacco and Corncob Pipes

Leaves of the sassafras are beautifully unique and easy to identify in the Blount County woods. When I do my daily walks with my old dogs, I think of Granny Anna's sassafras and rabbit tobacco. In the fall, around August in North Alabama, the silvery rabbit tobacco is seen standing tall in abandoned fields. As the hot summer ends, I become a little girl again, looking for Granny Anna's cures. There, on the bank near my house are three sassafras trees, and near them, standing tall, are clusters of silvery, smelly rabbit tobacco.

Blowgourd and 3 AM in the Morning

Blowgourd School

Around three o'clock one morning, I was wide-awake. In Granny Anna's collection of pictures, I made a wonderful discovery and a connection to my favorite local book. I heard of Blowgourd all my life, but never cared to find out about its history. Mother identified two pictures: one of Blowgourd School and another of Blowgourd Church. As I always do, I placed these pictures on the dining room table and looked at them as I started my day. Mother couldn't identify any of the people, so I thought I'd put them away in my idea folder. I walked outside to enjoy the cool, morning breeze and forgot about the pictures. When the cool morning gave way to the Alabama heat, I came inside to finish household chores. I decided baking a cake was more fun than tackling pictures. I found my recipe for an easy dessert. The house filled with the smell of cinnamon and apples cooking for the tasty Mountain Dew Dumplings. I sat at the dining room table for a few more minutes while the baking finished.

With another cup of coffee, I faced the pictures. The columns and windows on the school picture looked familiar, but there was no way I knew anything about the old school with the date on the back. It had been processed at Lollar's in Birmingham on July 18, 1935, ten years before I was born. My internet search stated: "Frank Lollar founded the photography shop in 1910." This was "the" place for photography needs in downtown Birmingham located on the fourth floor of the Lyric Building. I noticed more and more of my old pictures had "Lollar's

Birmingham" on the back. Finally, I refocused. Lollar's would wait for another day.

I opened my *Heritage of Blount County* and went page by page looking at schools. On page fifty-nine, I found my columns and windows. The school was Concord (Blowgourd). I never made the connection with Concord and spelled Blowgourd as Blow Gourd. Adding to my excitement was the name of the person who contributed the article, Jeanette Sherrer. I recently talked with her about Green's Chapel Cumberland Presbyterian Church and the Green family who donated the land.

At this point in my writing, it doesn't bother me to impose on people for information. Sometimes, they are excited to help, and sometimes, it's best to move on without them. Jeanette was willing to help in the past. I decided to impose one more time. She was again pleased to talk me, and I made an appointment to visit her with my pictures and my mom the next day.

Blowgourd Church

I went to bed thinking about my trip to Jeanette Sherrer's home on Green's Chapel Road. I was ready for this trip. That day, I drove slowly down the road with Mom reminiscing about who had lived here when she was growing up in the Blowgourd area. To welcome us, those wonderful old-fashioned petunias were in full bloom in front of Jeanette's house. They were like the petunias I remembered from my Aunt Pearl's home. If they love you, they'll come back to grace your yard year after year. To me, this was already a good visit.

After hugs and laughter, we settled down, and I put the pictures on her table. The conversation between these two Southern ladies was wonderful. I listened to them reminisce. I forgot my recorder and couldn't take notes fast enough. Mom went to first grade at Blowgourd School, and Jeanette also attended Blowgourd School. They talked about who might have been the teachers. Looking at our old school picture, they wondered if Edgar Robertson was on the far right. And maybe, could he be Louis Johnson in the middle, and could he a Head Boy in the front? Perhaps Ace Johnson's daughter was in the back as she was always a pretty girl. A mystery surrounded the church picture. They both remembered the old church but couldn't remember the denomination. They talked about Jeanette's dad, the well-known pastor, Homer Ridgeway.

As we continued looking at the old photographs, I commented on so many processed at Lollar's in Birmingham. Jeanette told me her cousin, Ada Clayton, worked at Lollar's, and it was "The Place" to have pictures developed. She talked about Lollar's for a while, and my curiosity about this business returned. Reasoning took over, I put Lollar's aside again in my mind. They resumed talk about the old church and believed someone purchased the land and building, torn it down and built a new house on the spot where the church was once located. I felt sadness for the loss of the two old buildings which were not preserved. I suppose we can't save them all.

We lingered around the table for a long time in peaceful conversation about things past. It was finally time to make our way to Oneonta. As we walked out onto the porch, I looked one more time at the petunias and came back to our modern world.

Chocolate Covered Fried Ants

Uncle Bud on Patrol

Until I got very serious about my family history, I thought I knew a lot about James Henry Johnson. Born April 6, 1926, he was my mom's brother and my Uncle Bud. He lived in Birmingham all my life and visited us regularly. Everyone looked forward to his visits. Always happy, we felt loved when he was around us.

On one of Uncle Bud's visits, he came by my house in Oneonta. My son, Bart, was a young fellow playing "Army" in the woods on the extra lot. I called Bart in for the day to clean his room. He was not happy about having to be inside or clean, and he told Uncle Bud he could "just run away from home and live in the woods and never have to clean a room." Uncle Bud asked him where he would live and what he would eat. Bart replied he would eat bugs, animals, and build a tree house.

I never thought about the running away again until Uncle Bud's next visit. He came in with a bag from a specialty food store on First Avenue in Birmingham. He had food supplies for Bart when he ran away. Of course, Bart was so excited to get a gift, but especially, a gift of food from this special person. I can only image what thoughts went through Bart's mind as he looked in the bag that day to find toasted grasshoppers and chocolate covered fried ants.

In Granny Anna's picture box were lots of fragile, aging papers with James Henry Johnson's name on them. These passed down to my mom. There were lots and lots of pictures of World War II soldiers with no names on them. There were pictures of death and war. I simply got all the pictures and papers about him put in a folder for later. My sentimental memories of him and the last years of his life kept me from finding the right words to start his story.

The information stayed in the folder for almost two years, waiting for me to find the perfect words. Yesterday, on a cold weather alert morning, I pulled out the folder and spread the contents across my dining room table. I knew his military records were in the folder, so I started with them, making copies of the fragile papers. There was so much to sort. I really didn't know what I wanted to use. During the day, I looked at the table, sighed, and walked away.

It was around twenty degrees outside the morning I circled the table again and sighed one more time. I sat down. My heart became heavy as I read about this eighteen-year old farm boy from Blount County, Alabama. He only completed the tenth grade and farmed sixty acres from 1943 until October 1944 when he entered the Army. He trained as a heavy machine gunner and ended up in the Philippine Islands for the Luzon Campaign. His commendations and citations are stated as: "Asiatic Pacific Campaign ribbon with 1 Bronze Star and Philippine Liberation Ribbon with 1 Bronze." He became part of the liberation of the Philippine Islands between the dates of October 1944 and September 1945. The military of Japan was driven out of the Philippines before their surrender in 1945.

During his service, he purchased pictures of the Philippines. "Kill the Bastards" was among his collections. After many internet searches, I found the picture but not the name of the photographer. Some references state, "it probably relates to the Bataan Death March where many American POWS were killed by Japanese."

"Kill the Bastards"

I found a very fragile letter dated February 19, 1945, signed by his dad, Albert Johnson. "If I can hear from you every day, I can make it," were my Grandpa's words to his son. "Maybe, this will be over by May, and I hope then all the boys can go home." Uncle Bud was honorably discharged on December 5, 1946. He lived to come home and celebrate another birthday in Alabama with his family.

He completed his high school education after the war and went on to attend Snead Junior College in Boaz. After Snead, he applied for a GI grant to attend Howard College. At the time, Howard College was located in the beautiful East Lake area. The college later became known as Samford University. He became a member of Ruhama Baptist Church. He had an apartment nearby before he built a house. He experienced many successes in his life, but he could not be victorious in one war. Uncle Bud battled alcoholism after his return from the war as so many other WWII veterans did. He often admitted himself to alcohol rehabilitation facilities in the Birmingham area. We visited and were supportive. It was the hardest battle of his life. He lost that war with alcohol the day he died from a fall while drinking. When his friend found him, Uncle Bud was in a coma. He never woke up. As I rode in the ambulance with him to the hospital, it never occurred to me he might die. He was my Uncle Bud, who had always been kind and happy when I saw him. He made my mom laugh. The fact he became an alcoholic did not change our love for him. In those days, we had not heard of PTSD. One of my editors, Rachel Dean, said the words I couldn't find: "Unfortunately, I've known lots of WWII veterans who just were expected to come home like everything was normal and literally 'soldier on.' Such a shame!" I sometimes wonder if the trauma of war started Uncle Bud on the path of alcoholism.

As for those chocolate covered fried ants, well, they stayed in my freezer for years, uneaten, but a gift from Uncle Bud.

Minuteman Stamps

In these modern days, the word "patriot" lost a lot of its old-fashioned meaning. I remember my dad was a proud supporter of his country and its way of life. My Uncle Bud believed in service to his country. I looked the word up on an online dictionary, "patriot -one who loves his or her country and supports its authority and interests." Its origins come from the Greek word meaning "fatherland."

When I found my Uncle Bud's Defense Stamp Album stored away in those old boxes, I started thinking about patriotism and the way the average person of the past supported the country. The Minuteman of the Revolutionary War stood tall with the American flag on the cover of this little album. On the other side was the American eagle and another flag in the background. The United States Treasury Department issued a

World War II Savings Stamps Book

series of war savings stamps in late 1942. They didn't earn interest like the World War I stamps. You filled them up and used them to purchase a war bond. The internet is full of old promotional posters for sale, or they can be found in museums. I found a poster that read: "Joan of Arc saved France-Women of America save your country-Buy War Bonds." During World War II, famous people like Frank Sinatra and Bob Hope made advertisements to market bonds.

Today, as I typed this brief idea about the Defense Stamp Album, I pondered the old word "patriot" for some time. With the unrest, violent behavior, and cruelty we hear about in the daily news, will we ever be able to achieve the past level of patriotism?

Frances Darnell Whited

A White Horse Named Trigger

Born March 18, 1933, Charles was the youngest child of Albert and Anna Johnson. Mom said he was born at the Roberts's house on Tuscaloosa Road. My memories of Uncle Charles are few, maybe because we were both young when he died, gone too soon for me to collect memories. Charles married Villa Dell McHan, and they had two children, Valerie and Charlotte. I have memories of a shop in Oneonta where Charles worked for Curt Thomas covering car seats. Valerie Redman, his oldest daughter, shared e-mails about her father and encouraged Villa to give us more stories about him. Valerie, Villa, and Charlotte now live in the beautiful North Georgia town of Ballground. The town is located near fields where the Cherokee people used to play stick ball, a rough game similar to modern lacrosse. It's an ideal area for thinking about old stories.

Valerie's e-mails about conversations with Villa gave me an insight into Charles's personality. He was what we in the South refer to as "tender hearted" and kind, especially to elderly people and animals. He was very meticulous about his appearance. Everything had to be perfect, and he never went out unless his shoes were cleaned and shined.

A wonderful quote from Valerie's e-mail said: "When I was born, he didn't want anyone to touch me. He was so afraid of dropping me, he held me over the bed just in case I fell. Mama said when she got pregnant with me he got sick on tomatoes. That's why I've always hated them. When Mama was pregnant with Charlotte, Daddy jumped out from behind the door and scared her. It caused her to bump into the door. He felt so guilty about that later. Mama and Daddy were just kids themselves. They were so young."

My personal memories are of his beautiful brown eyes, brown hair, and wonderful smile. I see that smile in our old pictures. My favorite picture of him finds him seated on a huge white horse on Old Tuscaloosa Road. There's no saddle, so we can assume he rode bareback. I asked my Aunt Villa what she remembered about Charles and the white horse. I was hoping for a long, detailed story. She said with a smile, "He probably just wanted it."

Charles was the baby of the family and possibly got almost everything he wanted. Mom said when he was little she called him her "Little Pear." It was a name from a children's book.

When I asked my mom about the horse and Charles, she laughed, and told me a brief story, "Well, the horse's name was Trigger, like the Trigger from the movies and Roy Rogers, the cowboy. Trigger and Charles were known around the community. It was said the horse was a very social animal and liked to visit neighbors. If he got away, he came back. Everyone knew he belonged to the Johnson boy. One day Trigger came back home and across the yard without his rider. There was Trigger, but where was Charles? Sometime later in the day, Charles was seen walking home down the dusty road."

Charles Johnson and Trigger

Mom laughed, and said, that's all she knew of the story.

I remember when this good looking, young, gentle man became sick. Since we were children, Jerry, Valerie, Charlotte, and I weren't told what was wrong. We knew something wasn't right. Life was more silent than usual. I remember Valerie and Charlotte spending several nights with us. Charles went to a Birmingham hospital and was gone for days. He came to our house. I was so happy he was home. I believed he was no longer sick. But, a seriousness settled in after that day, with little laughter. Charlotte became sick with a cold and spent the night with us. I was supposed to give her medicine that night. I dropped her bottle of medicine. The bottle seemed to break into a hundred pieces. Mom came into the room to find me crying. I worried about the cost of medicine. She told me we could buy another bottle. There are no memories for me about Uncle Charles after that night. Since I was a child of around twelve, maybe the gift of forgetting gave me the ability to cope with a loss of family.

On January 31, 1957, Charles died of Hodgkin's lymphoma when his adult life just began. At that time, there was no medical hope for a cure, only injections of morphine for pain. Years later, Villa built a house behind us on Tuscaloosa Road. My brother, Jerry, and I grew up with our two cousins living behind us. We played together, shared holidays, trips, visits to the storm shelter on stormy nights, and created shared memories. In today's world, cousins don't seem to have those shared memories, and sometimes they never meet. What a terrible loss it is for families not to share life, its happiness, and grief!

Jerry Grigsby and Charles Johnson

Chapter 4 - Footprints of the Green Family

It's time to step away from the Roberts and Johnson families for a while and look at the Green family, which is still alive and well in our county. (It is sometimes spelled Greene.) Over fifty names are listed in the local phone directory. Growing up, I knew I was related to the Green family, but I don't remember us ever visiting this side of the family.

My Granny Anna had a way of finding out about people, and I've been told by others their parents did the same as Granny Anna when they first met a stranger. First, she would say, "Who are you?" and then, "Where you from?" Giving the stranger time to answer, in the next breath, "And who are your people?" Back then, this was an acceptable way to find out about a stranger. My granny never met a stranger. She was going to find out about their people. She knew who she was, and she knew who her people were. Her mama was Martha Liberty Green, whose folks came from "Georgy," or as we know it, the state of Georgia.

My opinion of the Green family is simply stated. They descended from a bold and hardy stock that migrated from Georgia. As early settlers, they were immune to the inconveniences of wagon travel. They had independent spirits.

A healthy disregard for hard times was necessary. In a small wagon train, they followed their dreams down a dusty trail to Blount County, Alabama.

The Greens of Hall County, Georgia

There was only one picture of Thomas Benton Green in the picture boxes. It's been circulated around and used often by those writing about him. Mother didn't have any great stories. The one story she told was about "the chest." The history of an old wooden chest is part of the history of the Green family. Mom has it in her room. It is her treasure, made by Thomas Benton Green. When she speaks of the chest, it is easy to hear the affection in her voice. The chest had a long journey. It was first given to Martha Liberty Green (Roberts), and then passed next to Anna May Roberts (Johnson). It rests now with Mom (Martha Frances Johnson Grigsby). One day, it will move again to my little house on the hill.

My knowledge of this side of my family comes from internet searches, reading **The Heritage of Blount County, Alabama**, and contacts with relatives by phone or internet. According to combined research, Thomas Benton Green was born in Georgia around 1838. Another book, **Miscellaneous Confederate Soldiers from in and Around Blount County**, stated "Confederate Service Records reported Green enlisted as a Private in Captain J. G. Lister's Company D of the 55th Georgia Infantry at Gainesville, Hall County, Georgia on 16 May 1862."

In the comfort of my home, I read about his capture at Cumberland Gap on September 9, 1863. I followed his imprisonment in Louisville, Kentucky, and later, Camp Douglas, Illinois. There were around 540 southern soldiers who survived and were released from the prison at Camp Douglas. One of them was Thomas Benton Green. He was discharged on June 14, 1865, many miles from his home in Georgia.

In my mind, I created images of this Georgia man. We don't believe he was a slave owner. So why fight in this war? It turned brothers against brothers, fathers against sons, and ruined lives across the country. Men who were lifelong friends became enemies. In war, almost everyone loses, and sacrifices are made on both sides. I prefer to believe Thomas Benton Green, like both Union and Confederate soldiers, did what he understood to be his duty. He did what was asked of him by his leaders for he had nothing to gain!

Frances Darnell Whited

As each side returned home, history recorded in vivid photographs, the battle worn men. At the end, most likely, the weeks and months following were filled with fatigue, hunger, homesickness, and old potholed roads. Nightmares invaded their much-needed sleep. Mom uses the phrase, "My mouth is dry as a powder house." Was this a phrase passed down in a family who knew about powder houses to store gunpowder?

Like most Southerners, I know a good bit about the Civil War. What I don't know is Thomas Benton Green's journey back home to his wife in Georgia. Reading about his pension approval and medical examiner records, I know he injured himself from a serious fall off a horse, leaving his right shoulder in bad shape. I know it's a long walk from Illinois to Georgia. Maybe, he wore the remnants of his Confederate uniform, or maybe, he never had one. Was he traveling with other soldiers making their way back to their families? The roads most likely weren't safe for him to travel in the daylight. Where did he sleep? How many days did it take him to find his Georgia home? Had he heard of Sherman's March across his home state and feared his family might be lost to the war? I don't know the answers to these questions. I don't know his physical condition or the challenges he faced on his way home. Mom remembers hearing relatives tell the story about a family member finding a strange man in bed with Frances Green one morning. At first, no one recognized him. This worn, traveled man was her husband home from war.

In 1862, when Thomas Benton Green left for the hostilities of war, he also left behind a pregnant wife. His daughter, Martha Liberty Green, was born on October 25, 1862, while he was away. After his return, he removed his family from Georgia to Alabama. We can only

Thomas Benton and Frances (Moss) Green

speculate the reason he left. History records the harsh living conditions in Georgia after the Civil War. A sadness comes over me when I think of modern hate for the word "Confederate," a once simple word meaning joined by an agreement or treaty. I imagine old men like Thomas Benton Green want us to work things out peacefully and learn from history.

One early morning, I sat reading. I wanted to check on information about Lula Jane Roberts Pass, a sister of William B. Roberts. Lula married James Marshall Pass. The Pass family history opened doors to the migration of the Green, Horton, and Roberts families. I found George B. Pass, the grandson of Revolutionary War soldier Nathaniel Pass, married Frances Louise Green. Frances was the daughter of Isaac Green and Mary Matilda Jackson Green. Here was another way I was related to the Pass family!

According to Volume 5, "Sometime around 1870, Frances Green Pass left Georgia in the small, wagon train bound for Blount County. Frances's siblings, Leroy, Benton, Armilda, and Mary Green were among those traveling to a new home." This was part of the Thomas Benton Green's of Hall County story.

When I look at the surviving pictures of Thomas Benton Green with his wife, I see two very serious Southerners. I see the results of the war in the hollows around his eyes and gauntness of his face. The Bible is on a table beside them. Is it the same Bible in all their family pictures? In later photographs, I see the signs of joint damage in his hands. I notice they are not wearing wedding rings, but we know they are married. If we look closely, he is propping his right arm in these pictures. Was this because of the injury during the war? There comes a better understanding of my mother's love for the old wooden chest resting safely in her room. She knew its journey to her. We'll never know if this chest made the trip from Georgia in a wagon, or if Thomas Benton Green built it when he settled his family in the area of Dry Creek Cross Roads.

The story of the Green family could be a book of its own. I discover them scattered about the country and additional information becomes available with each passing month. I came across more newspaper clippings as I dug though the picture boxes. I found old letters with clippings tucked inside them. One newspaper clipping lead me out of

Frances Darnell Whited

Blount County to Alvord, Texas. For a while, we will leave Blount County and travel to Texas.

Another Green from Alvord, Texas

My knowledge about this side of the family was limited. I wasn't even sure about the brothers and sisters of Thomas Benton Green. I had less information about Frances (Moss) Green, his wife. Several old letters were sorted and placed in the bottom of a file as "not family." One day, I looked in the file and took out a letter dated 1942. I thought, "Someday, I will read it. Who are these Harrisons from Texas?"

While waiting in the doctor's office, Mom had a wordy conversation about the family and where they lived. I realized even though many Greens remained in Blount County, still more moved away. I began to find them in Jefferson, Tuscaloosa, and Cullman Counties. The letter from Texas might be family. The aged, yellow envelope had the right side ripped off. Cora Harrison, the daughter of J. I. Green, wrote to Martha Roberts of Tuscaloosa Road from Alvord, Texas. I learned from this experience not to be so fast to label old letters and photos as "not family." The old letter was worth reading and using in my stories. It tells of the loneliness of a pioneer of Alvord when his wife of many years died. It expresses Cora Harrison's feelings to her Alabama relative about World War II. It conveys her concern for the "Boys" in service. She tells us of an Uncle Albion. The letter brought with it a newspaper clipping from *The News,* communicating the death of Mrs. J.I. Green. I eagerly read the information about her family and mine.

At the time of this writing, I haven't made contact with a living relative in Alvord. With a smile, I think, it only means I haven't found them yet. Maybe, there were no male children to pass the name, or the male children only fathered daughters. Telling a little about this family only adds to the mystery and the quest of looking for small clues.

The research for the Green family may take some time. I have many questions about their journey to Texas and the roads they traveled. Perhaps, a great story with a family picture will come home to Alabama.

Frances Darnell Whited

Alvord, Texas
Nov. 20, 1942

Dear Aunt Martha,

Dad wanted me to write you about mother's death and sends you clippings of the paper. You probably heard it through Uncle Albion. Dad can hardly see to write, and he is awfully feeble and so lonely since mother is gone. He and Joe live together and Joe works every day and leaves Dad by himself. The fact is I don't get to go see him as much as I'd like to. We have a filling station and grocery store, and just the two of us, so it keeps us on the job. We have one child, a boy 17 years old. He quit school last term and has been working ever since. He has a civil service job in New Mexico over 90 miles from home. He works in office good, but everything is so high costs him to stay there. It is a big Army base. He is just crazy to join the Air Corps, but we don't want him to. He will be in the Army soon enough. Isn't this war awful? Do you have any boys in service? I would be so glad it could be soon over. Aunt Martha if you feel like it write a long letter and help to cheer him up. He is grieving himself to death, but I said he should be thankful he outlived her, because he could give her more attention than anyone else could. He is a dear old Dad and was so patient and kind to mother, said he enjoyed every minute of the 17 years he waited on her. We never could be good enough to him, and how I would like to do more for him.

        Write when you can
        Love from his daughter
        Cora Harrison

Mrs. J. J. GREEN BURIED AT ALVORD CEMETERY

Mrs. J. I. Green, beloved pioneer citizen of the Alvord community, passed away at her home here last Saturday evening after an extended illness. Funeral services were held at the Alvord Baptist church Sunday afternoon with Rev. Ross A. Smith and Rev. W. F. Mercer officiating. Burial was in Alvord cemetery in charge of Rhyne Funeral Home.

Sarah Jane Chambers, daughter of Mack and Mary E. Chambers, was born Dec. 7, 1859, in Blount county, Ala. She was married Dec. 14, 1879, to James Isaac Green in Blount county, Ala. To this union six children were born. She is survived by her husband and three children: Joe B. Green, Gus E. Green and Mrs. Cora Belle Harrison, all of Alvord; also by 14 grandchildren, a number of great grandchildren and by one great, great grandchild.

Mrs. Green had been a faithful member of the Baptist faith for 70 years, having professed faith in her Lord and united with the Missionary Baptist church in her community in Alabama when she was thirteen years of age.

The family came to Texas in 1902, locating at Alvord where with the exception of five years spent in Arkansas, they have lived ever since, and can properly be termed "pioneers."

Three children preceded Mrs. Green in death. All were grown and two of them were married. One son, Charles Terah Green, died in France during World War I.

Mrs. Green was a patient sufferer for many years. Injured in a fall in Feb. 1925, she had been an invalid ever since. Her health had been none too good for the past 30 years. Her husband was her constant companion during the long years of her suffering; and ministered to her with unfailing tenderness and devotion, doing all he could to comfort, cheer and brighten her heart and life. And how he will miss her, now that she is gone! Not only he, but all the rest of the loved ones and many friends and neighbors who have known and loved them throughout their long residence in this vicinity. The News joins their neighbors and friends in extending sincere sympathy.

Mrs. J. I. Green's Obituary

Frances Darnell Whited

Out in Oklahoma

The quest for the Green family again pointed me out of Blount County. Of the hundreds of pictures, I took my time finding the right ones to use with each story. Two pictures I really liked had no story. On the back of one was written, "Mother Hansard's 62nd Birthday, Mother and her chickens." I remembered seeing another picture of a bit younger woman with chickens all around her. The first question in my thoughts, "Would Mom know anything about this lady?" The next question, "Where did I file that other picture?" By this time in my writing, all of these old folks began to overlap, run together, and gave unexpected connections.

The picture was found in the huge Green file. With both pictures together, side by side on the dining room table, there was the "Ah Ha" moment. These were the same person. Mom decided it was her Grandma Roberts's sister, who she called Aunt Fannie. She was a Green, but that was all she knew. These pictures didn't want to be filed away as useless or unknown. They stayed with my ideas for later, often being in the way of some other idea.

Frances Green, Grandmother's Sister

I hadn't looked at my Ancestry.com account in weeks. On a day when the words refused to present themselves, I decided to see if anything of interest had shown up on that website. It was meant to be! I had an inquiry about my connection to Thomas Benton Green. I replied to an unknown faceless person. This individual gave me access to the Family Tree of the person whose first name was Cecilia. There in her family tree was the name "Hansard." There are lots of Hansard names across the United States. I could not find Fannie. I wrote again about my picture and the name on the back being Fannie. The reply was Fannie's real name was Mary Frances. I asked myself, "Was this the Mary who traveled by wagon train from Hall County with Thomas Benton Green and Frances Green Pass?"

Now, I have the beginning of a story. Again, I remember the importance of persistence. Sometimes, all it takes is determination, a small clue, and persistence. According to Cecilia's research, Thomas Benton Green and Frances E. Moss were married in Hale County, Georgia. They had a long list of children: George A, 1860; James I, 1862; Martha Liberty, 1862; Elia Luvina, 1866; Mary Frances (Fannie) 1868; Robert Leroy, 1869; Oliver, 1871; Arana, 1873; Albion Benton, 1875; and last, Thomas Lafayette, 1870. These names matched my list.

The Fannie Green in the pictures I liked so much was born on February 16, 1868, and died on February 1, 1962, in Pawnee, Oklahoma. She married James Henley Hansard. Census records indicate she lived in the Indian Territory of the Chickasaw Nation. Why did this family move so far from Blount County relatives? And, why settle in Indian Territory? I talked with Mom about their move to Oklahoma. She gave it some thought and answered, "Well, it could be they were looking for work. You know, they had those oil wells out in Oklahoma. People came from all parts of the world wanting to strike it rich."

Fannie Green, with her 62th birthday cake and her chickens, waited for a longer story. On this tropical storm morning, another e-mail arrived from Cecilia. I previously sent her pictures of the recent luncheon with the Dewey Roberts's family and invited her to the next get-together. My story for these two loved pictures began to come together. With thanks to technology and DNA, I found another relative in Clovis, California, a long way from our dusty Blount County roads.

I pondered the migration of this family from Alabama as it moved across the United States. They left behind their contacts in Alabama over time as they journeyed across the country. We Southerners often say, "Well, I'll be." This morning I said, "Well, I'll be, found another cousin, way out there in California."

I made that second cup of coffee and read the email from my new found cousin:

"Hi Darnell,

"I apologize it has taken me so long to respond. I was trying to get more information about the reason the Hansard family may have moved to Indian Territory in Oklahoma without much luck though. As far as I know, there are not any Native American ancestors. The DNA tests that both my brother and I took didn't show any Native American ancestry.

"My grandfather Chester Hansard died when my father Marvin D. Hansard was about four years old from Typhoid fever. My father did not have much information about his father's side of the family.

"Thank you for the invitation to the luncheon. It's a bit far for me to travel right now-I live in Clovis, California. Enjoy the photo of all of you-- looks like a wonderful group of women I would like to get to know! :) Cecilia"

Robert Huston Hansard Age 18 years

Again, "Well, I'll be" was my thought. I love the idioms of the South, I paused for a while and researched the meaning of the saying, "Well, I'll be." It's used as an expression of surprise or astonishment, especially regarding some recent revelation. The recent revelation of lost family may lead to more pictures and more stories of the Green, Roberts, and Hansard families, but it wasn't meant to end with these two pictures.

The name "Hansard" floated around in my memory of pictures from those boxes. While working on a different story, a picture of an interesting young man looked out at me. He stood in front of a tree with his hat hanging on a branch. I turned it over, and on the back, written years ago was "Robert Huston Hansard, age 18 years."

One more lost relative, one more mystery, and as I type, there are more questions. "How is Robert related, where did he live and die, and will he have his own story?" While looking back in the Green file, I found Jim

Hansard and Billy Horton witnessed the marriage of J. I. Roberts and Martha Liberty Green at the home of T. B. Green in 1886. Who is Billy Horton, and how is he connected? Is he a Horton relative?

This is the perfect place to tell readers the importance of putting information, as much as one can, on the back of photographs: who, what, where, age, etc. Research tells us to use a number one or number two pencil, write on the edge of the back but never on the front. Frances Osborn Robb, author of *Shot in Alabama,* spoke to the Blount County Historical Society in February, 2018. She made a powerful statement I will always remember, "Keep your photographs where you would feel comfortable spending the night – not a garage or an upper shelf."

While we wait, maybe there is a story forming for other relatives of Thomas Benton Green.

Who is Ona?

Fannie and James Henley Hansard

The name "Ona" was signed on the back of a yellowing picture. My son, Bart, and I worked hard to figure out the comment which disappeared slowly over time. Ona wrote, "This is Mother and Dad, if Mother knew I was sending it she would give me a whipping. It was taken last summer. /signed/ Ona"

A little further down, she added the comment, "Bessie might of sent you one like this, did she?" Here were two clues, Ona and Bessie. As I always did, I carried the picture to Mom. She looked at it for a while, then handed it back. She shook her head, and said, "I don't know those people." I asked if she remembered a relative named Ona. A simple word, "No," ended the questioning.

This was another picture I loved. The couple sat in their car, the top down, and looked like they were ready for a little trip. And, look at the running board...I could almost reach out and touch it. I imagined a ride down a dusty road in this car. I wore a big, wide hat like the one in the picture. The couple wasn't smiling, but I would, if I could ride in that car.

Like so many of those old pictures, I left it on the dining room table. I saw it during the day, picked it up, sighed, and moved on to something else. Another morning came, I made my coffee, circled the table, and sighed. But, this morning was different. The lady's face looked familiar. Had I seen another picture of her? Or was this my imagination? With the magnifying glass, I looked again at her face. I looked at the yellow, aging paper of the picture. At that point, I knew there were other pictures of this woman printed on similar picture paper. There was a moment of dread!

Would I look again in the boxes and boxes of pictures with no names? I drank my coffee and left the picture one more time.

It was about bedtime when all the questions about Ona came back to me. This time, along with the questions, came a possible answer. The face of the lady was a face I had seen. She had to be Fannie Hansard, Mom's Aunt Fannie who moved to Oklahoma! Joy of joy, I wouldn't have to look in those boxes because she was already part of a story. It was getting late, but with three clues…Fannie, Bessie, and Ona, I had a story.

Morning coffee and computer ready, the next day, I answered the question, "Who is Ona?" Ona Hansard is listed in the 1920 United States Federal Census. Household members listed are James H., Frances, Wesley, Bessie, Ona, Mattie, Jessie, and Huston. I'd been searching for Huston, whose name was on another picture. My only unanswered question remained unanswered, "Why did they leave Blount County?"

With these pictures, they continued to be a part of the Thomas Benton Green family of Blount County. With this brief story, they now have a place in family history. It makes me feel very happy even though I will never ride in the car with them. When I put on my big, wide hat this summer, I'll think of the folks who moved to Oklahoma.

Frances Darnell Whited

Waiting on Alvan and the Death of Grandma Roberts

Waiting in the doctor's office with Mom always gives me time to ask questions. Clarifying little details in the oral history is achieved. This day's long wait reminded me of my notes on "Waiting on Alvan." These were put aside because there were two Alvans in Mom's past, a Johnson and a Green. There were two different faces on the pictures. Also, there was Albion. Who was Albion? Had I confused the story, combined both men into one? Had she combined the stories? Because of the confusion, I put the pictures away without a story.

As we sat waiting, I asked, "Can you tell me about the Alvan who came from Birmingham on a bus when someone was dying?" Wrong question! I hadn't worded it right to get the story. Her reply was, "Well, Uncle Alvan came when your Uncle Charles died. The bus was late, and he didn't make it to the funeral. But, he spent the night with Mama after the funeral." Since that didn't get the information I was hoping for, I spoke louder and asked, "Can you tell me more about him?"

Albion "Alvin" Green's House on East Lake Blvd & 2nd Ave., B'ham

Mother tells the story of her Grandma Roberts dying: "Well, you know Alvan, he always wore a hat. There's a picture of his house somewhere. He moved to Birmingham, lived on Second Avenue in East Lake. He worked in a feed store, but I don't remember the name. When he was growing up, they lived down an old dirt road that went to the Blackwood's. When I was a kid, I walked to the old house. Nobody lived there at the time, and I went in the back door and looked around. There used to be another house where Alvan's Mama lived. It's near where the Bynum house was on the old road. It's now Highway 231."

Mother became lost down the dirt roads of her past and memories. She told me about all the old houses that have gone. "Mom," I said, "You told me a story about your Grandma Roberts and Alvan. She was dying." While she takes a few minutes to refocus, I wait patiently.

Albion Green, Anna's Uncle

The story finally comes. "Well, Alvan liked to come visit, and he liked to walk to Austin Creek Church. One time when I was young, he came up and wanted to walk over there. He asked me to walk with him. We got to the river, and the water was so high, we couldn't go across. We had to turn around and go back home. I think maybe the Greens donated that property to the church. (That's the first time I have heard that! Had she confused it with the Greens of Green's Chapel Church?) When Grandma was dying, she lingered for days. Alvan rode the bus up from Birmingham while she was dying. The bus stopped way down on the highway. Grandma heard it and said, 'That's Alvan.' He walked the rest of the way to Tuscaloosa Road. After he got there, Grandma lived about fifteen minutes. She was waitin' on Alvan to come home. You know, Alvan had a son named Milford. He had a daughter, I think, but I can't remember her. I think his wife was the daughter of Ed Posey."

A lot of information wove in and out of Mom's memories. I made notes on the back of the receipt from the doctor's office. We waited for over an hour that day. The rain fell pretty heavily outside. Mom watched the rain falling in the pasture across from the doctor's office. She started to talk again: "You know there's a picture of a little girl in a wheelchair. That's Grandma's sister. Grandma said she went to bed and was fine. She woke up the next morning and couldn't walk. I think she died young."

Mother told these stories with sincerity to pass on as authentic family history. And, who am I to dispute my mother's stories from long ago? Has she blended information? Time, patience, and documented information will untangle the web of ancestors. The Alvan of her stories is most likely Albion Benton Green, son of Thomas Benton Green. Over the years, the pronunciation with Mom's dialect changed the name. I am happy to have a few words for the "Alvan" who moved to East Lake and came when Grandma Roberts died.

As I'm closing the stories on the Greens, I wish to write about Oliver from Cullman and Lafayette from Georgia. I found Oliver's family in Cullman through Dr. Drew Green at the Cullman Museum. Thanks to him, I contacted Bob Jones. There will be more information thanks to Bob's research. His mother was Ruth Green

June 3, 1937

R. L. GREENE

Shortly after reading the week's issue of The Alabama Christian Advocate and talking with his family of news of his life-long friends he ministers of the North Alabama Conference, there entered upon rest Thursday afternoon, May 6, R. L. Greene, 67, from his home at 4324 Jackson Boulevard, Inglenook, Birmingham.

He was born in Gainesville, Ga., Sept. 26, 1870, the son of Thomas Benton and Frances Moss Greene, but removed to Alabama when he was two years of age. He attended Walnut Grove College, graduated from Blount College, and also attended Peabody. For twenty years he taught school in Blount and Jefferson counties, his last school being at New Merkle. He entered business at New Merkle in 1906, and for the sake of his children's education removed to business at Boyles-Inglenook in 1908. He married in Oneonta in 1893; Anna Clowdus, daughter of Wilson B. Clowdus and Violantte Powell, who was a pioneer teacher in Blount County. Their children, all of who attended Birmingham-Southern College, are: Merritt, business man of Birmingham; Mrs. Perry D. (Gladys) Scrivner New Haven, Conn., and Annalee, teacher in the Tarrant schools.

Surviving him besides his widow and children are four brothers—James Greene, of Texas, J. O. Greene, Cullman, and A. B. and T. L. Greene, of Birmingham and two sisters, Mrs. Fannie Hanson, of Texas, and Mrs. Martha Roberts, of Cleveland, Ala.

The deceased was a life-long member of the Methodist church, having been baptized by the sainted Rev. R. J. Wilson at Cleveland in his eighth year. He was long Sunday school superintendent and steward. He had many friends, and all knew him as a good man. He was a Mason and Odd Fellow. He had retired from business in 1936 due to ill health.

The funeral was held at Brown's Funeral Home, Norwood, at 2 p. m. Saturday, May 8, by the Rev. Dr. W. R. Battle, assisted by Rev. R. L. Baker and by the Rev. L. L. Hearn of the Boyles Baptist Church. Interment was in the Forest Hills Cemetery.

"The memory of a righteous is blessed."

This is written by a friend, and son of one of his former pastors, the Rev. Henry S. Matthews.—Charles D. Matthews.

R. L. Greene's Obituary

Jones, a daughter of Albion (Alvan). Bob found the grandson of Lafayette in Georgia. Recently, I found Elia Luviana died young and was buried in Cleveland. Is this the girl in the wheelchair? At this time, I can't confirm. By email, Bob told a wonderful story about our shared family. "My dad was born in 1934, so his memory was limited to Uncle Ollie and the youngest brother who they called Uncle Fay (LaFayette). Uncle Fay lived around the corner from Albion (Alvan) Benton Green in East Lake. Daddy has some recollection of going to the country in Blount County to visit relatives." He states, "I can tell you a good bit about our Green branch who moved from Blount Springs to Bessemer. Albion (Alvan) Benton ran a store at one point in Bangor. Daddy remembered a few stories about it. At some point, he worked for Birmingham Mayor, Mel Drennan, who owed the resort at Blount Springs. They were living there when the place burned the last time in 1915 and soon after, he moved into Birmingham where he continued to work for Mayor Drennan."

The story of the Green family is not finished, but we'll leave it with a newspaper clipping about the death of R. L. Green (e) in 1937. Sarah Miller, daughter of Dewey Roberts, mailed the clipping, and it ended up in the picture box. With e-mails and phone calls, more stories may someday be ready to tell. And so, today I wait.

Frances Darnell Whited

Chapter 5 - Footprints of the Grigsby Family

As we drive north of Cleveland, there is a new bridge crossing the Locust Fork portion of the Black Warrior River. Before this bridge, there was another concrete bridge, before it a bridge with trestles, and before it, another low-water bridge, now lost in time. Years ago, eighty acres on the right after crossing the bridge, belonged to the Grigsby family. There was a simple wooden, tin roofed house Vess and Annie McCarty Grigsby called home. Their children were Nina, Cora, Ethel, Carl, Clifton, and Odell. Of these children, only Cora and Ethel left Blount County after their marriages.

Odell, my father, often talked of arrowheads, which could be found when the ground was made ready for planting in the spring, but the Native Americans were removed years ago. The Grigsbys farmed this once Native American area and made a bare living. There were no frills. They knew the value of home-grown food. Everyone did their share of work in the fields. The women canned and nothing went to waste. A few pictures survived in Mom's picture box to document their life. A group picture under their big shade tree is a combination of Johnson, Bryan, and Grigsby families.

I never spent the night with Vess and Annie or heard their stories. Vess died before I was born, and Annie died when I was three. When I think of this family, I envision the women sitting in straight back chairs. They are under the shade tree shelling purple hull peas or shucking corn. I imagine Annie calling her family in from the fields. The adults follow an old familiar path leading them to the house. The small children stop playing for the evening meal.

The Old Tuscaloosa Road is believed to have passed in front of their home, then, curved on down to the river.

Searching for the Grigsbys

Odell, Darnell, Martha and Jerry Grigsby

Tucked away in the back woods inside a fenced area off Highway 231 in Cleveland, Alabama, is the Blackwood Cemetery. To my surprise, here is where I found the graves of Ira Emery Grigsby and his wife, Sarah Allred Grigsby. As far as I can determine, the Grigsbys are not related to the Blackwoods. Most of the Grigsby family are buried in the Austin Creek Baptist Church Cemetery. Maybe, these folks were friends of the Blackwoods, or most likely, lived nearby.

I found these ancestors by accident. I worked hours with cemetery books in the Blount County Memorial Museum looking for last names of known relatives. My dad, Odell Curtis Grigsby, spent years looking for the McCarty name but not the Grigsby, Easley, or Allred name. His mission was to find his connection to the Native Americans. In his thinking, Sampson McCarty and his wife were the important ones. My family tree has lots of empty branches, so I put Dad's information in a file for later and searched for the Grigsby side.

Mother remembered hearing "some Grigsbys" were buried near Five Points. It was not much of a clue, but it headed me down an old road to find a fenced cemetery. On a Saturday evening, Mom and I took a trip, driving old roads, looking for the place where some of the Grigsbys were buried. There, resting peacefully amount the trees of the Blackwood Cemetery, was part of the Allred and Grigsby families. We found Alsbury Allred, the son of Andrew Allred. There were no dates on the headstone for the wife of Andrew Allred. Her name was Levicey Easley Allred. Andrew Allred was not buried here. I walked around again and still no Andrew.

Ira Emery Grigsby (1852-1940), his wife, Sarah (1852-1917), and daughter, Alter (1872-1886), are buried close by. Why had Alter died so young? Mom never heard. Odell's father was William Sylvester (Vess) Grigsby, and these were his people. These were pieces of the puzzle, but there was much more to research. The Easley name carried me to the history of the Easley Bridge and Daniel Easley. The lost Andrew Allred left many questions. I checked the cemetery records at the museum for Andrew. He was not to be found. Where was he buried? Where I found him explained an end to a sad mystery which became part of another story.

The migration of these family members followed paths from Stafford, Virginia, to the area of Blount County, Tennessee. There was no oral history passed down to me. The silent past was a difficult challenge, but I wanted a story from their old dusty trail to Alabama.

With the help of computer research, I came to believe James Harvey Grigsby, born in 1811, was the father of Ira Emery Grigsby. James Harvey married Elizabeth Lewellen, and they had nine children: Louisa, John, Phena, Eugene Franklin, Phoebe Ann, William Terrell, James Columbus, Elijah Monroe, and finally, Ira Emery.

Any internet research is subject to corrections, but with that said, if I traveled across the country to find original records, it would take years. For my purposes, I've used a lot of online information about the Grigsby family. I found Ira Emery married Sarah Allred, and they had nine children: Ather, William Sylvester "Vess," Vider Lee, Seretta "Sudie," Benjamin "Ben," Ruell V, Della, Gus, and Fanella "Fonnie." William Sylvester was my dad's father. I heard Dad talk about Uncle Ben, Uncle Gus, Aunt Fonnie, and Aunt Vidie. We visited Aunt Fonnie in the little village of Town Creek, Alabama. She never married, but she came home to Blount County at her death to be buried in Dailey's Chapel Cemetery.

There was a surviving picture in Mom's box pictures of the Grigsby homeplace near the river. My granddaddy, Albert Johnson, stood with his arm behind his back and his hat on the chair. Granny Anna sits near a woman and an old dog. The lady near the dog is probably Annie Grigsby. I'd like to believe the young child in Anna's lap is the young Darnell, me. On the other side of Anna is Zinkie Bryan, who lived on the hill across the river. Behind Aunt Zinkie is Hazel, Clifton's wife, holding a child. Next to Hazel is Hannah, Carl's wife. I don't know the men in the back. There are bicycles leaning against the house. This picture puzzled me because Grandpa is not wearing overalls. He is in his Sunday best for the visit to the home of Annie Grigsby. Why was he dressed up for this day?

I heard the phrase, "When you don't have a destination, you can't get lost." I decided to look forward to the journey and the search for lost Grigsbys. Smiling, I thought, "I can't get lost because I don't know where I am going."

So Few Pictures

Who are these people with so few pictures and limited oral history? Stumbling and uncertain, where do I begin writing about this side of my family? Mother clipped an article from the local Blount County newspaper. It gave me a family picture from the time the Grigsbys owned eighty acres on the Locust Fork River near Blountsville. My daddy, Odell, told the story of the picture to **The Southern Democrat** writer, Mrs. E. A. Maynor. In another picture found by Dad, his sister, Cora, posed on the bridge with a big sun hat.

A Grigsby story passed to me was of a fire in Dad's childhood home destroying everything the Vess and Annie Grigsby family owned. With no home, they lived with community members, until another home was built. Daddy spent his later years searching for pictures and finding lost relatives from his past. The two sisters in the newspaper picture, Cora and Ethel, moved away from Blount County. Dad found Ethel Grigsby Hart in poverty in the coal mining country of Alabama. After Cora's death, her children were lost from him for years, but later found in the beautiful hill country near Mentone. He traced his mother, Annie, back to Carroll County, Georgia, and found records of his grandparents, Sampson and Isabella McCarty. He found Sampson born around 1814 in Edgefield, South Carolina. Dad searched without the help of computers.

Finding his Native American ancestors was the quest for Dad. He believed the story of a Native American grandmother who lived in Georgia. Other ancestors often overlooked. One day, I discovered Sarah Allred's mother was Levicey Easley, and her grandfather was Daniel Easley. This was a major find in my researching. We are descendants of the folks of the Easley Covered Bridge. Daddy would enjoy telling that tale.

Computers may change what can be written about this family as it branches out in places like Ancestry.com. The greatest loss is the pictures and the oral history, which cannot be replaced by an internet search.

Blount County Beautiful

The Aug. 30 issue of *The Southern Democrat* was barely out until Odell Grigsby of Cleveland stopped by the newspaper office to identify the bridge pictured in "Blount County Beautiful" in that issue and brought along the picture featured today to prove his identification.

It is the picture that was taken the day the new metal bridge was opened, about 1920 or shortly before. The bridge spanned the Locust Fork of the Black Warrior River south of Blountsville. Those are Grigsby family members lined up in the picture. Odell wasn't around yet, but reading left to right are his sisters and brothers, Ethel, Carl, Cora, and Clifton, and his mother, Annie. He isn't certain but believes his father, Sylvester "Ves," is leaning against the old Model T in the background.

Occupants in the car cannot be identified, but "it would be a pretty good guess that car belonged to either Dr. (J.S.) Wittmeier or Dr. (W.C.) Miles," Odell said.

"Ves" owned the property on which the bridge stood. The 80 acres he owned formed a horseshoe shape around the bridge area. The farm passed down through Clifton, Dr. Miles, and Wiley Gordon and is now owned by Pat King.

According to Odell and his brother Clifton, the bridge shown replaced a low-water bridge that often was closed as much as a couple of months at a time during rainy weather. The only transportation possible then would be through a covered bridge upstream a distance. He could not tell anything much about the covered bridge; if it had a name, he hadn't heard of it.

Odell told more about how difficult it was to get around when the water was up. Even when the water flow was normal, it was sometimes a task to get across. There were no sides to the plank bridge; you had to be a steady driver of a reliable team.

And, to think we complain today about inconveniences!

Others reading this development in the Grigsby Bridge saga undoubtedly will have some contributions to make to the bridge's history. If you know of any factor to fill the gaps, phone Odell Grigsby at 274-7355.

—Mrs. E.A. Maynor

Grigsby Family on a Blount County Bridge

CCC Camps and the Young Odell

**Odell Grigsby and a Buddy at a CCC Camp
(Odell is at the Right)**

My daddy told us he "spent time" in the CCC Camps when he was young. The Civilian Conservation Corps was a work program created as part of President Franklin Roosevelt's New Deal from 1933 to 1942. The Great Depression left young men across our country with no hope of employment. Searching the CCC websites, I found reports stating by March of 1933, more than 13.6 million were unemployed. The CCC information on the website praises the benefit of this project. Planting trees, clearing streams, and improving parks turned out better than being unemployed and hungry.

Committing to the CCC was a life-changing event. The enrollee most likely would leave his home area. Mom had no information about those days in Dad's life. I became very curious about his records and applied to the National Archives for his documents and paid for the research. It was a fast and easy process. In less than two weeks, pleased, I found a big envelope in my post office box filled with records. Daddy's first application date was May 11, 1936, with the processing location of Cambridge, Maryland. Daddy rolled up his CCC pants and went to work. It was pure manual labor, but these young men were given shelter, clothing, food, and a little pocket money. From what I've read, there was a small wage of $30.00 a month, but they only got to keep $5.00. The other $25.00 was sent back home to their family. Vess, Odell's dad, died in March of 1936, leaving his mom, Annie, with no income. Twenty-five dollars was a lot of money for her in Blount County.

The camp photo was probably taken on a cold day. Odell is on the right with glimpses of long-johns and rolled socks. His pants and shirt are a little too big. Those shoes look like standard issue! The tag Daddy wore has writing I can't read. Where are they going with the buckets?

Daddy always joked about his education, but he was proud he attended the little Joy School in the Blountsville area. His CCC records showed he only had a fourth grade education and left school in 1932 to work full-time for his father. It took him a long time to get the fourth grade education because he never attended regularly. This information, given by my daddy, may not be totally truthful. His lack of education appeared to be an embarrassment to him.

He never talked about the days in the camps. He just said he "spent time." A lot of the young boys from Alabama, school drop-outs like him, left their homes and spent time in the CCC. The ages ranged from approximately eighteen to twenty-five. World War II came, and these young men soon found new jobs: war against Germany and Japan. They "spent time" in foreign countries. They left their homes and families again, but not always by choice.

Odell married a pretty girl whose folks lived on Tuscaloosa Road. With the help of family, he built a little white house on the same road. Later, he built what he called a "Poutin' House." Old men know a 'poutin' house' is a retreat for the man of the house. Daddy smiled and said, "It's a place for poutin', cussin', and smokin'." Slowly, over time, with the help of GI resources, he gained more education. He became active in all things concerning his hometown. When Governor Guy Hunt visited Cleveland, Odell arrived with a big smile and a handshake.

Odell and Governor Guy Hunt

Frances Darnell Whited

Seasick and Overseas

Martha and Odell

When Mom left her home on Tuscaloosa Pike, she insisted I bring the chest Thomas Benton Green made. She wanted it in her room at the Magnolia House in Oneonta. The chest was covered in many years of changes, old paint, and stick-on paper. Ben Royal, a neighbor of many years, offered to restore it when I took all the stuff out of it. When I use the word "stuff," it needs a bit of clarification. This "stuff" included years of memories, objects, pictures, newspapers, and bits and pieces of belongings Mom could not part with for sentimental reasons. History from her past, whether valuable or worthless, filled the chest.

While cleaning it out, I found a copy of *Our Patriots of America, World War II, Alabama*. It was published in Winston-Salem, North Carolina, by National Patriotic Publishers after World War II. I've spent many hours reading the names, ages, and hometowns of the young Alabamians listed in the old worn book. I noticed the term "Overseas." Beside my dad's name, Odell Grigsby, and his first cousin, Claude Grigsby, was the simple word: Overseas. These eight letters changed the lives of thousands of young men and women in Alabama and our country.

One day while sitting with the book, I looked at the very back. Blank pages were left for soldiers or family to write information. In the 'Personal History,' I found both my mom and dad's handwriting. Since neither of my parents graduated from high school, they wrote the words as they sound to a Southern ear, not as they are spelled. It's a wonderful documentation of Daddy's personal journey during World War II. What is not written is how homesick he was. He didn't write about the seasickness he had for many days as the ship sailed away from his country to the Panama Canal Zone. He didn't write about his fear of not returning home.

The war brought economic expansions to help in the recovery from the Great Depression. I read approximately 300,000 Alabama men "donned service uniforms." I looked at the picture of the young Odell, so handsome in his uniform. I think about the tremendous courage these young people had. I think of those left waiting at home, hoping and praying, their loved ones would return from Overseas.

Odell returned home to Cleveland and struggled to find a job after World War II ended. He worked for Ralph Hunt at the feed store. They made meal, and he delivered it. He worked for Sidney and Ercy Bellenger building roads. He finally got a job at Hayes International at the Birmingham Airport. He became a fireman and continued to work there until he retired. He is credited with starting the Volunteer Fire Department in 1968 in Cleveland. He put out fires. Maybe, it gave him some closure after the fire from his childhood.

The journey of life has fascinating connections. My dad often talked about Ercy Bellenger and his days building roads. I knew Mr. Ercy because of Dad. Mr. Ercy's home on Tuscaloosa Road was only two houses down from our house. I walked past it more times than I can remember. I made another connection to Mr. Ercy. I chose Beverly Ellis, who I had known for years, to read and edit this book. She already knew about my terrible spelling and grammatical errors. Beverly's daughter, Rachel, with her background in English, also helped. What I didn't know about Mr. Ercy was Beverly married his grandson, Bill. Mr. Ercy was Rachel's great-grandfather. She left me a note at the bottom of an edited page. "I can't believe he ended up in your book! That's so cool!" As I typed the corrections, I, too, thought it was cool! I wish I could tell Dad about this connection. He would have stories about Mr. Ercy for Rachel. She would love to hear them!

Dad talked of building roads. He sometimes spoke of being "Overseas," and he said he might want to see the Panama Canal Zone again. He mentioned it again one day and I told him, "Dad, I'll pay for you a trip to see it again. I'll go with you. You can tell me more about it." He didn't hesitate, and said, "I'll just stay here."

First Sunday in May

When April rolled around each year, the talk began about the First Sunday in May, and then, the third Sunday in June. The First Sunday in May is Decoration Day at two important cemeteries where the Grigsby and Johnson families are buried. The third Sunday in June is Decoration Day at the Cleveland Cemetery by the Methodist Church where the Roberts family graves are all near the front. Decoration Day is a tradition in the South. Flowers are placed on as many graves as you can afford to decorate. In April, it's important to decide how to afford decorating so many graves.

Austin Creek Baptist Church

The two cemeteries for May decoration are miles apart. Austin Creek Church, in the Blountsville area, is where my dad's family is buried. My mom's folks are buried at Green's Chapel near Cleveland. As a kid, there wasn't a choice about <u>IF</u> you were going to Decoration Day. You went every year. You went on Saturday to put out flowers. You went on Sunday to look at everyone's flowers. It was a time to visit with old friends and family and wear your new clothes. Sometimes, there was "dinner on the ground" because there were no tables. Years later, the tables came, and much later, the fellowship halls were built.

Preparing for Decoration Day took a lot of planning on my mom's part. Daddy was just an excited mess of instructions. Then, came the clothes. We dressed appropriately for both days. My brother and I received new clothes and shoes for Sunday. Meals were cooked in advance. The car gassed up. All the uproar over long dead family seemed to me to be a stressing event.

If we drove the Blountsville route to Austin Creek, we passed Fowler Springs. Daddy told us one more time of getting water from the spring and about the old church. We passed the white house across from the spring. I dreamed of owning such a beautiful place so carefully maintained. Dad's brother, Carl, had a cotton field on the left just past our left hand turn. Uncle Carl knew how to "witch" for water.

Fowler Spring Missionary Baptist Church

For those who don't know about witching for water, I'll elaborate. If you dig a well, first, you must know where to dig. Around Blount County, there were a lot of folks who knew how to witch for water. Uncle Carl had the gift! Some people called this gift for the unexplained process "dowsing," and still others called it "divining." Some people believed, and still believe, this to be a supernatural power, and that is for others to debate. My Uncle Carl used a forked twig, from a certain tree. He walked around until he felt the pull on the branch. Where the twig pointed down, allegedly water was below.

We go back to the road, and a little further down from Uncle Carl's, we dodged a huge boulder for years. It jutted out in the center of the road. Daddy told us about it being there when he was growing up, too big to be removed. Each trip, he told the same story about attending Joy School. Before our right hand turn to the cemetery, there was an old store in the middle of nowhere!

Sometimes, we took the Swann Bridge route. It meant going over the river and up the hill. We passed "Little Ed" Bullard's mother's house on the left. Her mother was Aunt Vidi so Ed's mother and Dad were first cousins.

Frances Darnell Whited

Green's Chapel was below Cleveland over another bridge on property, which once belonged to the Green family. Mother thinks her uncle, Tyre Green, donated the property.

As children, my brother and I weren't eager to hear about the coming of First Sundays. It was a time of agitation! All the flowers had to be ready before the Saturday event. There were a lot of dusty roads to be dealt with in traveling. The rush to get to two places on the First Sunday in May was less than a happy time for us. The most stressful year was when Daddy decided to make headstones. The graves, marked with field stones, needed to have markers with names on them. It was the year to make homemade concrete markers for Vess and Annie Grigsby, his father and mother. Tactfully describing my dad's personality is complicated. I can carefully state he was a bit high strung. Getting the concrete markers ready for that First Sunday in May, well, it pushed Daddy over the edge. He was more than the term "high strung." Mother enlisted the help of my calm-natured, Uncle Bud. Vess and Annie got their headstones. Lately, I thought about real markers with all the important information. My sentimental nature would not allow me replace the markers made that April.

Money was always hard to come by in those days. By the grace of our Creator and the strong will of my mother, everything came together. The four of us showed up in our new clothes. We always had flowers for everyone. One year, we learned to make homemade flowers from old worn out stockings. Another year, we learned to cut and put together beautiful flowers created from crepe paper. Some years, we cut flowers from every yard around and added wild greenery. There had to be flowers for all the graves of these loved ones who had passed.

The First Sunday in May can be warm. My memories are wearing a new summer dress, made by my mom, and being cold. I got new sandals for the summer in April. My toes were cold all Sunday. My brother had his little pants and shirt with new shoes. We were afraid to play because we might mess up the wonderful things with green grass stains or dirt. We just stood around looking polite. We were Odell and Martha's kids. We didn't get into trouble on First Sunday. After the May event, decorating in June was a breeze, only Mom and I were involved.

My mom and I still participate in First Sunday in May with a little help from my son, Bart. He needs to learn the tradition. We tell him the names of those who have gone on before us. We plan the flowers we are going to buy in April. The Saturday before the First Sunday, we put them out. We'll pass the spot where Joy School used to be and think of Odell telling us, "That's where I went to school." We'll place the flowers on each grave and talk a little about past Decoration Days. Mom said this year she hoped we returned next year.

I've learned this tradition all my life. I plan to carry it on after Mom has gone to be with those we have always respected with our flowers.

Frances Darnell Whited

Hummingbirds

Each year, I clean those bird feeders, mix the brew, and get ready for the hummingbirds to make their way back for a drink of sweet, Alabama sugar water. As humans, we too have our annual trips and traditions. Flipping through my follow up notes, I found a reminder: Don't forget about Fowler Springs. My daddy would not want me to forget about Fowler Springs. If you take a left hand turn off Highway 231, a little beyond the river bridge, going to Blountsville, you'll find a country road named Fowler Springs Road. Growing up, it was another dusty road my dad loved to travel. No matter how slow he drove the car, dust rose up behind it following like a red cloud. When he traveled in his later life, he shared lots of stories about this road.

Joy School

If you lived in Blount County all your life, you probably asked the question, "Is it Fowler Springs or Fowler Spring?" Well, I won't help you with that answer. On the sign in front of the church, it reads, "Fowler Spring Missionary Baptist Church. In *The Heritage of Blount County, Alabama, Vol. 5,* the church is called Fowler Springs Missionary Baptist Church. In the local telephone directory, it is listed as Fowler Springs Baptist Church. My Daddy called it Fowler Springs…so I will always call it Fowler Springs.

When I was a very young girl, we loaded up on Sunday morning to go to church at Fowler Springs. Reading about the beginning of this charming little white building, I found it started after World War II, with a meeting held in the old Joy School. Curtis Bowerman and Odie Johns were veterans who helped with the organization. Daddy knew both these men, and he loved taking Joy School. We always passed the Spring in front of Mr. Fowler's house on the way to church. It was a very dependable source of water in Dad's day, supplying humans and animals with sweet, spring water. Dad would say, "It was the best water I ever had. We'd just move the wiggle tails out of the way." Dad said he learned years later those wiggle tails were baby mosquitoes, and they carried malaria. While he was away at war in the Panama Canal Zone, he learned a lot about wiggle tails.

Some days, we drove down the dusty road to see Uncle Carl. He knew how to make the sorghum syrup Dad loved. We made a left turn before we got to the church to go see him. His house was on the left, past the Bowerman house. On we went, with the dust cloud following. Years passed, and Uncle Carl moved closer to Austin Creek Church: a longer drive, more stories, and more dust. That huge rock was still in the middle of road. I learned to drive out there on the backroad with Daddy crying out, "Watch for that rock!" Further on was an old building. It's still there, the wood turning black with tall grass all around.

There was a picture found in Mom's boxes of Joy School students. It had no names on it. All those young faces were left unidentified. I wish a young Grigsby boy named Odell was there on picture day. That is doubtful. Another find in the box was an article from ***The Southern Democrat***, dated September 5, 1984. It was written about attending the old Joy School Reunion. Mablean Edwards, sometimes called Mable, wrote the article. She and Dad were first cousins. Her father was Ben Grigsby. When they got together, they loved to talk about the old school days.

Joy School Student Body

Sometimes, twice a year, I make this sentimental journey, down the now paved Fowler Springs Road. One day this year, I drove to take pictures. As I drove to the spring, I thought about the hummingbirds coming back each year for the sweet, Alabama sugar water. On this trip, I

Frances Darnell Whited

stopped my car and walked to the spring. I felt the cool spring water. I imagined young Odell Grigsby as he came back. He moved the wiggle tails aside and drank the sweet spring water…the best water he had ever tasted.

Aunt Fonnie's Story

In September 1984, Mable Grigsby Edwards, the daughter of Ben Grigsby, wrote a letter about her visit to her Aunt Fonnie. Mable had been working on the Grigsby family tree. At the time, Fonnie was the last living child of Ira Emery and Sarah Allred Grigsby. The following is Mable's story of her visit to Aunt Fonnie.

"At the time, my Aunt Fonnie Grigsby was in the hospital at Decatur General, 1984, having undergone major surgery. At age ninety-three, she had never been to a doctor but one time in her life up until this sickness struck. Last Thursday morning, I gathered up what I had on the family tree, put it in my purse and went to spend the day with Aunt Fonnie in the hospital. She was feeling much better when I got there. I told her what I had on the family tree. We enjoyed the day so much. We started with her grandparents coming by ox wagon with everything they had in the covered wagon. They made the trip from somewhere in Tennessee to around Five Points, Alabama. It was getting late in the afternoon. My great-grandfather was hoping to come to a house so he could get some fire. He made camp for the night as he had seen several trails leading different ways."

Mable's story continues, "He started out on one trail after another in search of finding fire so he could cook something for his family to eat. After going several trails, he came to a house. They gladly gave him a big chunk of fire. He didn't care to tell them he wasn't sure he could find his way back where he was camped. So, he asked the Blackwood boys if they loved to hear anyone play a fiddle. They were thrilled to go back with him to hear him play the fiddle for them. While looking at the date on my grandparents' and aunt's monument, I saw this large flat monument. The name was Blackwood, and it said, 'First settlers of Blount County.' I wonder if they were the ones my great grandfather got the fire from. My grandfather died at eighty-eight, so we do not know if he was born when his parents came from Tennessee, as there were several others older than him. When the nurses came in, they enjoyed hearing us talking. They would like to have stayed. Aunt Fonnie said it was one of the best days of her life, as we had brought back lots of memories."

Mable visited the Blackwood Cemetery in Cleveland before her visit to Fonnie Grigsby.

After reading the letter Mable wrote, I thought about my visit to Blackwood Cemetery. At the time, I wondered why the Ira Emery Grigsby family was buried in that cemetery. Maybe, the Blackwoods were the ones who gave fire to the new Blount County settlers. I'd like to believe that.

An e-mail from Terry Grigsby Hufnagle, another descendent of Ira Emery Grigsby, made me smile. Her question, "Did you know Era Emery made his own casket?" No, I certainly didn't know that. Apparently, Terry's research found he was a casket maker!

My dad owned one picture of an older couple positioned behind a wooden chair. On the back of the picture was written, "Odell's Grandma Allred." The man was unidentified. Was this the Sarah who married Ira? Would she have heard the story about the big chunk of fire? Unfortunately, everyone who could answer this question has passed away.

Odell's Grandmother Allred (Man Unknown)

In the same envelope was a handwritten three page document. At the top of the first page is written, "Grigsby-Dailey," but it doesn't tell who wrote the information. This was family research before the time of computers, and it is a worthy inclusion in my stories. I am honored to have found one more family story of my folks as they travelled down to an old trail in Blount County. It is almost time for my evening meal, and as I walk to my kitchen, I had a new appreciation for my electric stove. I turned the knob, and the warm heat for cooking was ready. How wonderful! I didn't have to look for fire!

A Handwritten History

Filed away in Dad's research was a handwritten history of the Grigsby family. At the top of the page, it states, "Grigsby-Dailey." There is no author's signature to credit the individual. After reading it over, I came to believe it was written by an ancestor of Columbus Grigsby and Mary Jane Dailey. This is not my story, but a story given by another ancestor. It seemed to add more details to the Grigsby family history.

The writing states, "James Harvey Grigsby was born in Tennessee about 1811, according to census records. He married Elizabeth Lewellen, also born in Tennessee, about 1812. During the early days of the marriage, they lived at Cherokee, (Colbert County) Alabama. In the early 1840's, they moved, along with their four children at that time, to Joy, Alabama, located north of the Warrior River between Blountsville and Cleveland in Blount County, Alabama. This was a one day trip by ox wagon. The family remained in this part of Blount County, where James H. was a Methodist minister and preached at churches in that area. James H. and his wife are buried at the First Methodist Cemetery in Blountsville, although the graves are marked only by field stones. Family sources say the family included nine living children, six sons and three daughters, also two or three who died, later two were adopted. Census records do not agree completely with family reports of children."

The writer gives the names of the children with little bits of extra information as follows: "Louisa Grigsby was born around 1845 in Tennessee. This child is listed in the 1850 Blount County census although not remembered by the family members. She perhaps went by another given name later. John Grigsby was born around 1837 in Alabama. No other information, except he was killed in the Civil War. Of the four Grigsby brothers who entered the War; John was the only one who did not return."

We follow the notes:"Phena Grigsby was born around 1838 in Alabama. Shown in census records, but not in family records. Franklin Grigsby was born around 1840 in Alabama. Married to Unicey E (Betty) Watkins. Family reports they lived at Somerville in Morgan County. William Terrell Grigsby was born January 5, 1845 in Alabama. He married Mary J "Molly" Watkins (sister to Betty) on the same date as Betty, July 26, 1865. William Terrell died in 1938 and is buried in Nectar Cemetery in Blount County. J. Columbus Grigsby was born around 1896 in Alabama. He married Mary Jane Dailey. They had one living child. Elizabeth was born in Blountsville on September 24, 1867.

The family later separated, Mary Jane and her daughter moved to Arkansas, and Columbus, then, reportedly went west. The daughter of Columbus and Mary Jane appears in Jackson County, Arkansas in 1883 where she married Thomas Paul Clifford,

Sr., in Jacksonport, Arkansas. Elijah Monroe Grigsby born December 27, 1849, in Alabama, married Mary A. Rickles. "Lige," as he was called, and his family moved to Monette, Arkansas, and lived with a John Montgomery there. He is reportedly buried in Austin Creek Cemetery in Blount County."

Dad told the story years ago about his Uncle Marion who walked all the way to Arkansas. He never knew why his Uncle would walk so far from Alabama. Today, I ask, "Was he looking for his Arkansas relatives?"

The hand-written history ends with a family tree of Columbus and Mary Jane. Someone took the time to write little things known about the family of James Harvey Grigsby. I'll place this old yellow handwritten history in my Grigsby file and wonder who took the time to record these details. It was important to them, and they passed this valuable information to other members of the family.

**Phebe Ann (McCarty) Grigsby
and Francis Marion McCarty**

A Trip Back in Time

Yesterday, I believed I finished with the writing of what I call my first book. All the stories were written over a period of two years and were in the hands of folks for proofing and editing. It was finally out of my house and off my dining room table. I was at peace with the process. It snowed and iced the day before, so I felt no need to drive into town. I settled down to restore order to the files I used. In the McCarty file was a big white envelope. It was labeled in Mom's handwriting, "McCarty Keep." It hadn't been opened in years. I hadn't written much about these relatives. When I tried to get all the picture boxes sorted out and label the photographs, this envelope went in the file for later.

Sampson McCarty

That day, I emptied it onto the dining room table. A trip back in time began with each piece of paper. I wasn't sure about the emotion I felt. Was I thrilled or agitated? What was I going to do with this? Here on the table were pictures and documents which would add to the history of the Grigsby, McCarty, and even Allred family. I emailed a friend, who was helping me with the editing process. I told him I found more information for new stories, and I wasn't sure how I felt about it all. His reply gave me courage and direction, "Of course, it's par for the course. Newly found information negates half of what you've believed for years. That's what is known as the genealogical law of deliberate adversity." Laughing, I thought about it, and decided to label this phase of my writing as deliberate optimism. Now, I'm optimistic about where the road leads me.

My first morning cup of coffee was almost empty, as I looked again at all the information. My dad would read each piece and been happy with his findings. He'd be pleased with the letter from Snellville, Georgia, written by Donald Henry McCarty, Jr., in 2000, addressed to Robert A. Scott of Warrior, Alabama. I don't know how he came to have the letter, or if he made contact with these people. What I do know from this information, it confirms what I thought I knew about Sampson McCarty, Dad's grandfather. He was born in Edgefield County, South Carolina, and died in Marshall County, Alabama. It's believed Sampson descended from Michael McCarty of Edgefield County, whose father was born in County Cork, Ireland. Attached to the letter was page seventy-three, copied from *Early South Carolina Settlements*. Reading this information, I note mention of a pension application made by Isabella (Tolbert) McCarty. Memories came back of documents my dad showed me over twenty years ago. Were they filed with McCarty information? The realization I might spend the rest of my life proving all the work of other people was overwhelming. It was time for a second cup of coffee and clearing my thoughts.

At the table, I sat and read while Miss Molly dog rested at my feet. I sipped the warm brew and told her my concern for all this mess on the table, and she listened. I told her Christmas was coming, and we might want to eat at the table. Her interest was heightened by the phrase, "eat at the table." Miss Molly is not keen on writing, but she's very attune to all things related to food. We sat for a long time as I sorted and read.

The picture of Sampson McCarty is a rather large black and white photo, not an original. As I studied it, I saw my dad's features reflected in this older man. He looks a bit harsh, as did my dad in later years. I found the stack of documents for Isabella's pension. To prove she was entitled to a pension, she presented evidence of her relationship to Sampson, and the story began.

Isabella Tolbert lived in the same area of Carroll County, Georgia, as Sampson's first wife, Elisebeth Bird (probably Elizabeth Byrd). The first wife died on Easter Sunday in 1873. Sampson didn't wait long to marry again. In October of 1873, he married Miss Isabella Tolbert. It was her first marriage. He told Isabella he was born in Edgefield County, South Carolina, and later moved to Augusta, Georgia. He ran a beef market there for years. He left Augusta and went to Burke County, Georgia, for several years. He then came to Carroll County with his wife and five children and

Footprints in the Dust

settled down with his family near Isabella's mother. He told Isabella he served a year in the Indian War under Captain Isa McCrary in John Howard's Battalion of Cavalry. Sampson died at the age of seventy-three. Isabella, with the help of William B. Roberts and Ida Blackwood of Cleveland, began her documentation for a pension. Isabella's attorney in Washington, D. C., was Joseph H. Hunter, documented with a post card dated September 12, 1895. On Joseph Hunter's envelope was stamped, "No pension—No Fee." Another post card from the Department of Interior, stamped Indian War, gave her Pension No. 6393, established on July 27, 1892. The information ends there. Did Isabella receive her pension?

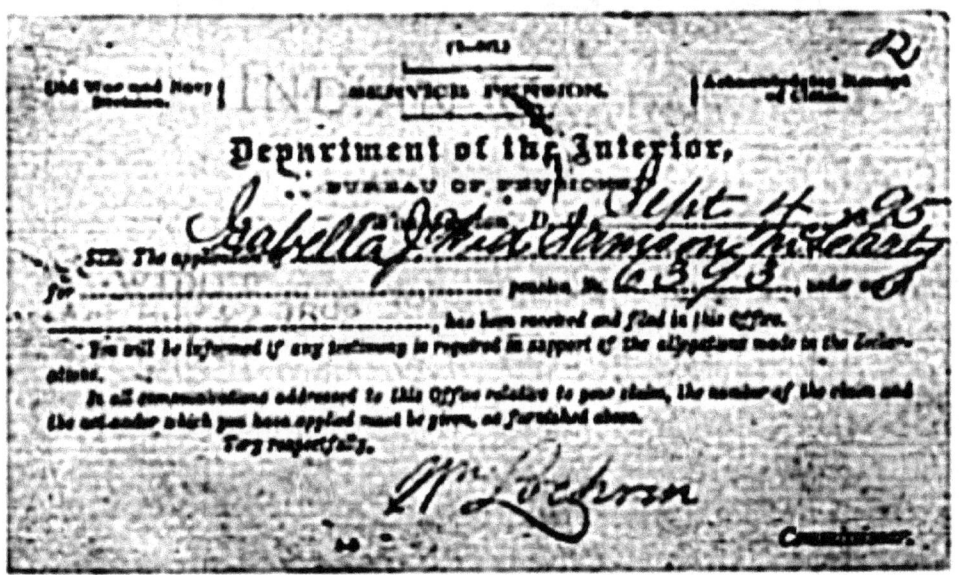

Indian War Pension Approval

In the white envelope was an enlarged photo of an aging Isabella. She's posed on the fence wearing her bonnet. At the gate, I saw a large dog and right outside was a little puppy. This woman owned dogs. I think we shared an interest in canine companions. I told Miss Molly about the dogs because she has an interest in them. Isabella left Georgia with Sampson and their family and moved to North Alabama before she settled in Blount County.

Isabella McCarty

This trip back in time has not answered all my questions about the McCarty family. Instead, it added more. I wonder what roads they took and think about the difficulties of travel back then. What were they looking to find in Alabama?

Maybe, that's what writing is about: First is a question, and then, we look for an answer. Often times, we don't know where we're going, and that's alright. You can't get lost if you don't know where you're going!

Chapter 6 - My Footprints

When I reflect on stories and books I read and loved, I suppose I came to believe telling stories is easy. The stories I told Bart and others in Blount County came easy, and I am comfortable with them and my audience. Once I undertook this, I simply started writing as I would speak. I was shocked to see the words in written form did not match my idea of what I was really trying to say. I had two binders of stories which made perfect sense to me, but I found others did not share my view or enthusiasm. Oh, they liked the stories, and the historical accounts were all well-received, but that was about as far as it went. A friend pointed out, more was necessary than just writing something down and believing that was sufficient.

Once I was over the surprise of meeting the reality of the situation, it became apparent I had sort of a chronological order to the stories, as well as a grouping of tales of the four main families. A bit of shuffling around, and placing old photographs with their stories, and I finally found me looking at my footprints in a fresh light. I am truly a product of my times, as my parents and grandparents were the products of their times. Like it or not, I am as I am because of both the people and the times. Writing these stories has been a cathartic experience, the extent of which would probably driven all thoughts of creating this book from my head, had I known what I was getting into.

Frances Darnell Whited

A Girl Searching for Family

Darnell and Her Bear

I began my search wondering, "Who is this Blount County girl searching for her family? Does she have stories, old newspaper clippings, and old picture boxes?" Well, when I started trying to write this book, I don't think I knew much about this girl. Now, I know her better. There really are stories to tell, for she has clips of newspaper articles, and she has boxes full of pictures, postcards, and letters.

I grew up in a little white house on Tuscaloosa Road. Neither of my parents graduated from high school. Even as a child, I knew I wanted an education. I knew I wanted to go to college. I struggled to overcome poor grammar and spelling. By sixth grade, I achieved more formal education than either of my parents received. I graduated from Cleveland High School in 1963, and began my college studies Snead Junior College in June of that year. I met an Army brat, Budd Rainey, the same summer. He left for Amarillo, Texas, while I continued on the college path in Boaz. We married in April of the following year.

I saw what the lack of education did to people and families. After my marriage, I continued at LSU at England Air Force Base. Then, LSU at Alexandria, Louisiana, and next, I moved on to Auburn University. My son, Bart, was born while I lived there. I dropped out of college for a while. We moved back to the mountains of Blount County, and I eventually earned a B.S. degree from UAB. A Master's Degree followed. Then, one day, I enrolled at the University of Alabama for a post-graduate certification in Administration. Just for me, I took a few writing classes with the beloved writer Margaret Searcy. I left Blount County early on Saturday morning for the eight o'clock class with Mrs. Searcy at the

University of Alabama. I had a professional career of twenty-five years at Oneonta City School. During those years, I was an elementary library media specialist, an assistant elementary principal, and elementary principal. My heart remained in the elementary library, and I spent my last years there with children's literature.

It was the fall of my seventh year of life when all my ancestors' pictures began to "speak" to me. Those pictures had been with me in childhood. My little brother and I sat on the floor, prowling through pictures boxes. We recognized our folks in these photographs. We knew Mom's Grandpa Isaac built the house next door. We heard the tale our little house on Tuscaloosa Road was built by my daddy and family members out of surplus materials from an Army Camp.

My stories began as a little girl in this small, but sturdy, white house that kept us warm in the winter. Old Tuscaloosa Road was there. The woods and fields of my ancestors were all around me. The mountains of Blount County were in the distance.

Frances Darnell Whited

Barefoot Little Girl Toes and Chicken Business

Often, I remind myself of going barefoot. I look at the shoes in my closet. I have great respect for a good, attractive pair of shoes. I suppose that came from my childhood. Taught from a very early age, I took good care of my shoes. You didn't mess them up as there was only one good pair for all special occasions. Wearing that pair meant no running wild in the fields, no kicking rocks, or playing in dirt. You didn't wear your good shoes on an ordinary day. They were given away to relatives when outgrown. In the warm months of Alabama, going barefoot was a common thing. The soles of my young feet became thick. They withstood a lot, with the exception of bee stings.

Visiting family was a popular event in my childhood days. We often visited Jay and Zinkie Bryan who lived near the bridge going to Blountsville. I called them Uncle Jay and Aunt Zinkie. Zinkie was really Ezinkie. She was the daughter of Joseph W. Roberts, whose father was W. B. Roberts. So, of course, we were family.

Anna and Zinkie, Barefoot on the Old Tuscaloosa Road

It was fun to visit their home. They always seemed happy to see us. There was laughter, and we could play with other kids. They had a big house compared to ours and a well on the back porch. The water bucket and dipper were on a shelf. Their chickens ran free in the big wide yard, and they roosted at night in the smelly chicken house. We played in the yard but did not go down to the river below their house.

As a young girl, I never thought about the going barefoot most of the time. I have a picture of Granny Anna and Aunt Zinkie under a shade tree on Tuscaloosa Road. They are both barefoot. It was a way of life. I suppose, I thought everybody else did the same. Around our place, we didn't have free-range chickens. There were no problems being barefoot except for those honeybees. It was different when we visited the Bryan family. I remembered to find old shoes to wear if I were going to play in the yard. In the excitement of going for a visit, I often forgot those old shoes, leaving me barefoot.

Free-range chickens lose their feathers everywhere. They do their chicken "business" wherever they please. Picture in your mind, running and playing, and stepping in chicken business! When you step in a fresh spot, it oozes up between your toes, all white and black. Mud squishes between your toes, but it doesn't feel or look the same. You know it the minute it happens, but it's too late. It's there as you look down at your five toes: chicken business. That quickly ended my playing. I went to the back porch. There was a bucket of well water. Next, I hung my feet over the porch and poured water slowly over my toes. The misery of chicken business devastated me. That it happened to me again was terrible and reduced me to a 'porch person.' There, I sat alone. After despair and cleanup, I settled into my routine of sitting on the back porch steps. The idea of stepping in that stuff again was too much for my little girl feminine nature. I sat and looked toward the river. My daddy grew up across the bridge. I guess he sometimes sat and looked at the river, too.

One day, Aunt Zinkie took pity on me and showed me where the doodlebugs lived. Those tiny, gray, hard-shelled little insects became my entertainment. From that day forward, if I were barefoot, I looked for doodlebugs in her backyard. With a broom straw or a thin weed, I moved from hole to hole and turned the straw. I said the words, "Doodlebug, Doodlebug, come out, come out, your house is on fire." I watched the little bugs come out to the top of their dusty homes. I loved to call up the doodlebugs. It was a game I played while looking down at my clean toes.

The original pictures for my story belong

to Allan and Susan Bryan. The lady with the two children is Zinkie's mother, Mattie Posey Roberts Smith. The young man is Hancel Roberts and young lady in the beautiful dress, Ezinkie (Zinkie) Roberts.

When I drive to Blountsville, I look to the left before I cross the river bridge. Zinkie's old house is gone, replaced by the beautiful home of Allan and Susan. It's a wonderful picturesque house on the hill with a good view of the Locust Fork River. I've never seen any chickens feeding in the yard.

As I go over the new bridge, I laugh as I think of the chicken business between my little girl toes and doodlebugs responding to my chant. I thank Uncle Jay and Aunt Zinkie for these wonderful memories.

Days in the Cotton Field

(Photograph courtesy of the Blount County Memorial Museum)
Cleveland Cotton Gin ca 1950

Growing up, I spent many days in the cotton fields around Cleveland and Blountsville. For years, Blount County children got out of school in September for "cotton picking." I thought every school in Alabama did. My friend from Woodlawn didn't even know what I was talking about, getting out of school for cotton picking was funny to her. She laughed at the idea and had never been in a cotton field. For me and many other people, it was an honest way to make additional money for school and family. We had to pay for school books back then, and it was a real hardship on some families.

My Grandpa Albert taught me how to pick cotton in a field on Tuscaloosa Road. Grandpa "carried" two rows, picked with both hands, and drug the big "pick" sack behind him. He told me, "You'll never amount to nothin', if you can't pick with both hands." He instilled this lesson in Mom as well. She could pick with both hands, "carry two rows," and pick around two hundred pounds a day. She made my pick sack, a much smaller version of hers and Grandpa's. I never reached the goal of two hundred pounds a day. If we picked early in the morning, the dew made the cotton a little heavier. One day, we started earlier than usual. Mom picked over 200 pounds, and I, finally, celebrated the goal of 100 pounds. Being weary, hot, and smelly was part of picking cotton. Resting wasn't an option since we were paid by the pound.

There was a cotton gin in Cleveland then. It was built to last with thick, heavy wood floors. In those days, a gin was an important part of the community. In cotton season, it might operate around the clock. Daddy worked there for a while. It was before he got his job at Hayes

International at the Birmingham Airport. He helped unload cotton. When we visited Daddy, there was a strong odor associated with ginning cotton. It flowed from room to room in the big, dark building.

The smell of the cotton field remains in my memory. It can't be described accurately to someone who hasn't spent hours in the hot Alabama sun, dragging a sack behind them. Those big white bolls, with their long locks of cotton down rows, make a pretty picture. When I look at them now, I can still feel the pain in my back. The unique smell comes back. It is the smell of cotton poison, dust, hard work, body odor, and oppressive heat. It's not a bad smell, merely the smell of the cotton fields, laborers, and families working together.

Some things I watched out for in the field were: spiders, snakes, packsaddles, cockleburs and saw briars. My daddy was afraid of snakes. A stick on the ground could make him jump in the air. Mom and Granddaddy didn't seem to worry about any of these. I got bitten by a spider in Uncle Carl's field in Blountsville. The field was overgrown with cockleburs and saw briars making a good home for spiders. We didn't go to the doctor for a spider bite: Mom put an Epsom Salt poultice on it. It swelled, ached, oozed, and finally, one day, it was gone but never forgotten.

The packsaddle was dreaded by everyone. It ruined your cotton picking for days. It's a really colorful caterpillar that becomes a moth. There are hairs on its body that secrete venom. It loves to spend time eating cotton leaves. These many years later, the old fuzzy things are interesting to read about from my safe, air-conditioned home. Yes, the smell of the cotton field comes back to me as I type.

Mom and I picked a lot for Mr. Hunt in the fields going toward Nectar. They were on both sides of what is now Highway 160. Mom used old gloves with the ends cut out to cover her hands and fixed a pair for me. It helped little. She packed our lunch with things that wouldn't spoil in the heat. Everyone drank water from the same bucket. We had no ice, but the warm water was really good after being in the hot sun for hours.

Small children often went to the fields. Even when my brother was too young to pick, he usually went with us. If you were too young, you did not get into trouble. You never played in the fields, didn't bother the pickers, waited for lunch, and then, 'quittin time.' A shade tree, if you could find one, was the place to stay.

At the end of the day, it felt like pure happiness to go home and rest. If you picked all day, your hands were sore from the sharp tips of the burrs. We combed cockleburs out of our hair and cleaned the saw briar cuts. Mom cooked the morning before we left for the fields. Our dinner at night consisted homegrown vegetables.

My brother and I shared a bedroom with twin beds which had cedar headboards. Summer nights were hot and humid. We opened the windows and hoped for a breeze that seldom came. We owned one rotating fan moving the warm air from one side of the small room to the other. We talked of our cotton picking money. What would we buy? I wanted material for a new dress which I would make for school. I learned to cut fabric and sew at an early age. We turned the spindles on the headboards of our beds and made squeaky sounds. The fan hummed softly as we drifted to sleep.

There are more stories about picking cotton waiting. If you grew up on the back roads of Alabama, you probably have a tale yourself of days in the cotton fields. When I drive to Guntersville, north on Highway 75, I see a cotton field with its long green rows waiting for the bolls to open. A machine picks the cotton and leaves a lot behind. Mom said in the old days it would be picked up, not left to ruin. That was Christmas money for her and her brother. Today the O'Shields, Hunt, and Tidwell homes are seen near the fields where cotton used to grow on the road to Nectar. I smell the field in my mind, sigh, and smile.

On occasion, I listen to the words from the song by the group Alabama, "Walking in High Cotton." In the South, if one is 'walking in high cotton,' times are good. The cotton is high, and the price for the sale of those white locks is high. Randy Owens's voice fills my ears: "We were walkin' in high cotton, Old times there are not forgotten, Those fertile fields are never far away." I wonder if Owens picked cotton because the song feels from the heart. I listen again and realize how much the song relates to me. Nostalgia and a bit of melancholy comes over me. For brief moment, I feel a homesickness for those days. It must be the song. I surely don't miss picking cotton!

Frances Darnell Whited

The Outhouse and the Old Milk Cow

Darnell and the Outhouse

When I started writing these stories, finding a real "outhouse" was a problem. In a picture of me as a little girl, there is an outhouse in the background at the Roberts's homeplace. In the Deep South of the 1950's, a lot of folks walked out their back doors and found them. Many tales have been written about this backyard necessity. Winters were cold in them. In the spring and summer, every imaginable insect came to live there: Wasps were among the worst. By fall, there was a smell that can't be described in polite terms to someone who never used one. "It's time for the lime" said by a user!

When I was around ten years old, our outhouse was in the fenced pasture behind our house on Tuscaloosa Road. The house and farm next to us belonged to my mom's grandparents. It passed down to family members. It had an outhouse not in a fenced pasture. My great-aunt Pearl lived there by herself. It didn't get a lot of use, and it might not have toilet paper.

Inside our fenced pasture lived a very unhappy, large old milk cow. My folks said she was a good old girl and wouldn't bother me. To get to the outhouse, I carefully, very quietly, opened the gate. I ran across the pasture hoping not to disturb her. She seemed to have the best hearing of any animal. I looked for her. I'd be about half way to the privacy of the little house when she started across the pasture toward me. Safe inside the little box of a building, I had my private time. Afterward, it was a 'watch and see' for me. Where was the cow when I wanted to leave? Was she outside the door waiting for me? Did she really just want to be friends? No, she did not want to be friends!

Footprints in the Dust

One day, after an escape from the little outhouse in our fenced pasture, I came to a conclusion. The old girl and I just didn't like each other. After that, many times I made the walk to the outhouse of my Aunt Pearl. It was nice to open the door to old fashion petunias instead of the old milk cow.

Daddy had a little problem with the old girl when he tried to milk her. She switched her tail a lot. About the time the milking started, Daddy got hit by the swishing tail. He had a seemly bright idea to cut the hair off her tail. He thought the slap wouldn't be as bad, so the old cow got a haircut. Unfortunately, when she swished her tail, it was like being hit with a rock.

Finally, the old milk cow was gone, and she wasn't replaced. Daddy grew vegetables, and the milk was delivered to the front door in a bottle.

Frances Darnell Whited

Whispering Pines and Bee Stings in Clover

As a child, I watched the honeybees busily working in the clover patches. In those days, there were lots of honeybees and white clover. My brother and I learned to watch for clover patches. A patch was an area with a lot of clover. We walked barefoot most of the warm months when clover was in bloom. If we were lucky that year, we had three pairs of shoes: one for winter, one for spring and summer, and another for play. They were usually a little too big when they were first bought, in case we had a growth spurt.

When school was out for the summer, there was no television or electronic devices to entertain us. We didn't have a lot of toys. There were no children's books in our house. We played with paper dolls cut out of the Birmingham newspaper. Old teddy bears fought for a while. If it were warm enough, we went outside.

Valerie Johnson, Jerry Grigsby, Charlotte Johnson, Darnell Grigsby

We played with our cousins, Valerie and Charlotte, almost every day. They lived in the little house behind us that was built after Uncle Charles died. At night, there were no street lights. When the lightning bugs came out, we watched as they blinked on and off. They were everywhere, waiting for children running with an old jar to capture them. A recent e-mail from my cousin Valerie said what we all felt about playing. "In my mind, we must have played together every day in those woods…they were like a magical forest."

The outside world was a source of magic and full of adventure for the four of us. There was a worn path to the pine thicket. We played "The Ground is Poison." We climbed trees with confidence, swinging from limb to limb, bough to bough. I read one time our original Alabama forests were once so expansive a squirrel could travel from Georgia to Mississippi without touching the ground. We didn't know about those squirrels as we bent pine trees and never touched the ground. We built towns with dusty roads on the ground and built houses from little sticks. We made "Mud Pies." We didn't wear shoes to play, instead we went barefoot.

As children, we knew the pain of bee stings, but we played without looking for bees. We were always running, wild and free. It was too late when the bees were remembered. The kid who runs the fastest, runs ahead of the group. Anyone following remembered to look for bees. Those behind knew when the sting was felt by the fastest runner. The scream is so loud. The worst is not over because the bee's stinger may be left in the foot. It's torn from the bee's body at the time of the sting, usually leaving the barbed venom sack stuck in the skin. Depending on how allergic the person is, there can be a serious problem. The foot will turn red, swell, itch, and become very painful.

I was highly allergic to honeybee stings and usually, the fastest runner. I've stepped on a good many bees, and I learned about the pain and swelling. A bad reaction meant two to three days of not playing outside. The pain and discomfort lasted a long time. Mom's cure was good old Epsom Salt. It was the family miracle compound, a cure-all, found in the average home. A poultice concocted of Epsom Salt, flour, and water was placed on my foot and wrapped in clean rags to hold it in place. For days, no running wild in clover for me!

Scattered about the sides of the road to my house are clover patches. We don't mow those areas when the clover is in bloom. It's left for the little bees. We live in a world with less and less clover patches. We almost destroyed the helpful honeybee. I don't use pesticides and watch for the bees to come back to the clover. On a good day, there will be a few little ones working the clover blooms.

Watching the bees, I know I won't take my shoes off and walk in the pesticide free clover patches. The magical memories of childhood came back and with respect for the flying insect, then, I move on to other thoughts. Leaves rustle gently down my dusty drive with the pine trees standing tall. The pines whisper today as they did in my childhood. I think of the country music song, "Whispering Pines." Honeybees and whispering pine stories are disappearing in Alabama. With a sigh, I feel the kiss of the warm sun on my face. Old times and old memories return as I make my way to the front porch.

Smiling Musicians, Joe Rumore, and WVOK

Joe Rumore and His Backup

Growing up, there were always smiling musicians, 'pickin' and grinning,' in our front yard on Tuscaloosa Road. While working my way into the depths of my mother's picture box, I found an old photograph of a group of smiling musicians. Of the musicians who were in and out of our home, this group was different. They looked professional, as if they were recognized for their talents. The microphone read "WAPI" on it. On my next trip to visit Mom, the picture came with me. When I asked Mom who they were, she sounded surprised I didn't know. "Well, that's Joe Rumore. Mama listened to him every day." Enough said. If you listened to the radio in Alabama back in the 1950's, you knew Joe Rumore. He was radio history in Alabama.

Looking back at the history of radio, we appreciate the importance of this means of communication. On December 7, 1941, the Japanese bombed Pearl Harbor. People across our country gathered around the radios for news. "And where is Pearl Harbor?" asked by many. President Roosevelt spoke to the country with his "Fireside Chats." Radio carried us away from Blount County with news from all parts of the world.

We didn't have television in my early years, so we listened to a lot of radio. I don't remember WAPI, but I remember WVOK. It was a staple in our life. Joe Rumore came into our home every week. We knew him and his family as if they were part of our own. We probably bought Golden Eagle Syrup because it was advertised on WVOK.

My curiosity took me to the computer to search for Joe Rumore. As I read the dates, I wondered if Joe Rumore was the one who told us Hank Williams died on January 1, 1953, at the age of twenty-nine. On February

Frances Darnell Whited

3, 1959, radio broke the news of the death of Ritchie Valens, J.P. Richardson (the Big Bopper) and Buddy Holly in a plane crash. Waylon Jennings lived because he gave up his seat. Radio was a voice in our daily life, bringing the good and bad of the world into our thoughts and daily life. The Grand Ole Opry filled our house on Saturday night with Minnie Pearl and Little Jimmy Dickens. We listened silently, in fear, to the news of the Cuban Missile Crisis, and waited for the words, "It's over."

Joe Rumore, WVOK, and radio were our connection to music and the world outside Blount County.

Terminals and Trains in Birmingham and Oneonta

When Jerry and I were growing up, we took Saturday trips with Mom and Dad. After many low paying jobs, Daddy's job at the Birmingham Airport gave the family more money for trips. We all crowded into the front seat of the best car. Car sickness was the dreaded motion sickness that attacked both my brother and me if we rode in the back seat too long. It needed to be avoided if we were going to have a good trip. We didn't have seat belts then, so packed tightly in the front seat, we left Tuscaloosa Road behind us for a day out.

On that Saturday morning, we went to Birmingham. Mom had cousins living on First Avenue South, so we assumed we were going there. Lucille and Ida were fun to be around. My brother and I called them "The Laughing People." Obviously, they laughed a lot. Uncle T. C. also lived in Birmingham. Maybe, we'd go there. It seemed like a long trip. The roads were paved but curvy and narrow. Daddy told us about the "old" road he remembered being a lot worse with more curves and lots of dust. We saw traces of it as he drove.

Our first stop was East Lake Park. In those days, it was like a carnival. There were rides for children and a beautiful lake in back. We didn't stay long, and Dad drove into Birmingham on First Avenue North. We passed Woodlawn High School, which I described as beautiful. I imagined going to school in that magnificent building. It was an amazing sight which went with me into old age.

Watching the tall buildings of downtown Birmingham come into sight was wonderful. The best view of Birmingham was crossing what Dad called the "via dock." We sighted Sloss Furnace on the left. Daddy told us about pig-iron and the blast furnace. He also said it was haunted by a man who fell into an open furnace. That really got our attention! We already knew about ghosts from Grandpa Albert's stories. Off to the right was the Birmingham Terminal Station. It became like Woodlawn High School in my mind. The image of driving down Fifth Avenue, looking at the terminal, stayed with me. I asked Mom about the trip. I wondered if we were picking up someone from the terminal, someone who had actually ridden a train. Instead, she told me, "We just wanted to look at it." Look at it we did, long enough to burn the images of the grand terminal into my memory.

Some Saturdays, our family took trips to Oneonta. There was another train station here. There were grocery stores in downtown Oneonta when I was a kid. My folks drove into town on Saturday for things they needed. When I was old enough, trusted by my parents, I held my little brother's hand and walked across the street from the grocery store. We stood, looking at the station. Maybe, it wasn't as grand as Birmingham, but it was another train terminal for our memories. Daddy called it 'The Depot.' When he said the name, it was "D Pole."

We stood without saying a word. If a train came, the rails made a strange sound. Then, the rails brought the train. Whistles blew, and the train passed to parts unknown. Walking away, with our backs to the station, I always felt a little downcast to leave the place that fascinated us both.

As an adult, I had the opportunity to ride some famous trains in Europe. I saw grand stations in London and Paris. Nowhere did I find a train station that impressed me more than the great terminal of Birmingham and the small station of Oneonta. Seen through the eyes of a child, with my little brown-eyed brother holding my hand, these were the grandest train terminals in the world.

While writing this story, I talked with people about the need for the perfect photograph of the Birmingham Terminal Station. There wasn't a picture of the terminal in our picture boxes. Several people gave me copies of their favorite photo of the terminal. The only problem with the "favorite" picture of the terminal was the photographer and date was not on the picture! I've searched but the source of my photo is unknown. There are many similar to it on the internet. I am grateful to the photographer who took this view of the great, domed building and "The Magic City" sign. It is a treasure from the past.

In the summer of 2016, I attended a meeting sponsored by the Blount County Memorial Museum in the newly restored Little Brick Church. The guest speaker was Marvin Clemons, the author of *Great Temple of Travel*. His book documents the end of an era in Birmingham, the trains of the past, and

Birmingham Terminal Station

the destruction of Terminal Station. It was a trip back in my memories. I crossed the First Avenue Viaduct of my past as I listened to Mr. Clemons speak about the magnificent Birmingham Terminal Station. I imagined "the grand dome rising majestically above the Birmingham skyline" as he spoke of the terminal. In his book, Mr. Clemons writes of the "weed-grown lot with a for sale sign" where the building once stood. Who were these people with so little vision they destroyed this classic landmark?

After the meeting, I drove to the Recreational Park in Oneonta. There was the little depot, restored for Blount County. We appreciate the vision of local people who saw its historical value. In my thoughts, I walked with my brother to the little Oneonta train station of my memory one more time.

Frances Darnell Whited

Skunks around the Pot

If you grew up in the county, you probably have a story about a skunk. Why would I want to write about skunks around the pot? We all know by definition, "Skunks are mammals known for their ability to spray a liquid with a strong odor." What you may not know is the truth about skunks. Skunks will parade around a black wash pot at night. There was no picture of a skunk in the picture box. I can't imagine why! The cute picture used is an internet picture and the photographer is unknown. A brave person got near these two animals. I thank them for the amazing sight. I, for one, would never try to photograph these cute creatures.

We don't take pictures of skunks!

Now, this is a true story. My Grandpa Albert loved telling about the night he looked in his backyard and saw skunks circling the black wash pot. My Granny Anna washed their clothes in that pot on wash day. With modern washing machines, it's hard to imagine filling a huge cast iron pot with water drawn from a well, starting a fire under it to boil water, and stirring the clothes in lye soap. This was a hot, complicated laundry process. I was always told to stay away from the boiling pot, and stay out of the way of the person attending the pot. Tales of terrible burns made an impression on me, and I honored the request.

My parents lived about two city blocks from my grandparents on Tuscaloosa Road. In the 1950's, Cleveland was a very rural country, backroad town. A lot of wild animals visited backyards at night. Long after our bedtime, Grandpa banged on the door. He woke the family up to come see the skunks circling the wash pot. He walked in the dark up the dirt road to have someone witness what he saw. Dad and Mom left quietly, walking with him back down the road. To my great, everlasting disappointment, I didn't get to see this. Someone had to stay behind with my sleeping little brother.

After that speedy, silent walk, everyone found a safe place to watch. The skunks were still there circling the pot. Why they were going around and around, we may never know. It made for interesting front porch talk for years to come: the night the skunks paraded around the wash pot. In the future, when Grandpa told this story to listeners, he always added Odell and Martha saw it too. This made the story true because he had witnesses!

Many years later, my son and his new wife moved into the old Johnson house. They planned to restore, remodel, and live in Grandpa's old home. The house was surrounded by ten acres of land. Some of the land was used for growing vegetables for the family. Deer, possums, and raccoons left their tracks in the tilled soil. We never thought about Grandpa's pot skunks.

One night, my son heard an strange noise. He soon learned there were skunks under the house. The skunks sprayed, and an awful smell began to fill the rooms. There was no way to escape what happened. The smell burns into your nose and memory. Needless to say, it took tremendous effort to remove the odor from everything inside the house. Some months later, my son moved into a house in Oneonta. Westside Baptist Church used the house for its services until a church was built. The house remains on the Old Tuscaloosa Road, now called Tuscaloosa Pike. Do the descendants of those skunks still live on the hill in the pine trees overlooking the old house? Mom and Dad were sure the skunks of my son's day were relatives of the skunks circling the pot when I was a little girl. I inherited the black wash pot. I've not seen any skunks parading yet. Grandpa Albert would say, "It's a true story. The night the skunks paraded around the pot."

Frances Darnell Whited

Dishpans and the Drought

My Granny Anna washed her dishes in a dishpan and rinsed them in another dishpan. The wash water was warm because the pans sat on the wood burning stove. When the waters got a bit cloudy, Granny walked out the back door and poured the water on any plants that needed water. Sometimes, she tossed it flying across the yard. One huge Elephant Ear plant loved the dirty dish water.

I hadn't thought about those dishpans until October 2016 when Alabama went days and days without rain. Our state was in a Stage 4 Drought, a frustrating and dangerous weather experience. I heard a local man, each morning and evening, pumping water for his animals from the river below my house. He gathered huge containers on the back of his pickup truck and ran a pipe into the river. One day, he didn't come back because the river was only a few stagnant puddles.

My childhood memories of the importance of a good well started coming back. There was very little "city water" in Blount County back then. All the people I knew owned a well. They depended on a good well in the backyard. My grandparents' well was in a covered building behind the house, and it never had a pump. They released a long, round bucket down the well, drew it back up, and emptied into another bucket to carry into the kitchen. I remember another bucket on a shelf on the back porch with a dipper. Everyone used the same dipper. My Aunt Pearl's well was conveniently located outside the kitchen on the covered porch. At her house, we lowered the bucket into the cool water, pulled it up, and emptied into the shared bucket with a dipper. There was no waste of water.

I never gave much thought to the pulley and rope device. This was just the way we got water. Later in my childhood, my dad got a pump for our well. Miracle of miracles, we didn't have to draw water anymore. There was one disadvantage, however, the loss of prime. Prime is an important word. It should be spelled in all capital letters, PRIME. Did I know how to prime a pump? No! A Google search had the following steps: "Turn power to pump off. Remove bushing with gauge and vent plug on opposite side of gauge on casting. Pour water into pump until water comes from the vent hole. Reinstall vent plug, top off water at gauge and reinstall gauge and bushing. Turn power on. Open faucet or hose bib at pump to bleed air from system."

Now, reading these few steps makes the process appear simple. Trust me, it is not! First, the pump is pulled out of the well and that takes some strong men. Next, where are the men going to get the water? Therefore, water must be brought to the site. Need I go on?

There was always a lot of drama when the pump lost its "prime". Sometimes, all attempts to prime the thing failed, and the pump was winched up and out. I never stayed around for that exciting episode of life. It was better to disappear and wait for the incident to be over. A lot of choice words echoed back and forth between the men folks as they debated an assortment of best practices. At some point, water was again delivered by the pump that had been "primed."

Albert Johnson's Ice Tongs and Darnell's Well Bucket

Memories of Uncle Carl pulling into the front yard with containers came back. Daddy told us, "Carl's well's dry." This was serious business. Carl's containers and our extras were filled with water for his cooking and drinking. A bath became a luxury.

Recently, a woman in the grocery line complained about her dishwasher being broken. Of all things, she washed all those pots and pans by hand. I had been writing about priming pumps. I couldn't be moved to sympathize, so I listened politely. What would she do if the water stopped coming into her house?

Today, I walk to my kitchen, push a button, and fresh, cool water fills my glass. I imagine the words my Grandpa would say about this modern miracle. He would be amazed. As the drought of 2016 progressed, I often thought of my granny's dishpans. The plants were green by her back porch. I got a renewed respect for the liquid we call water, flowing daily into our houses. One day, I even thought about buying a dish pan. And, next year, a rain barrel might be a good idea. I got the air-conditioning service man to run the overflow drain line to my flower bed. I bought a galvanized well

Frances Darnell Whited

bucket, the long cylindrical type, at a local antique shop. It hangs on my back porch, a reminder of the sweet well water from my past and the treasure we call water.

The Economics of Our Thanksgiving Turkey

One summer day, Dad came home with a baby turkey which we were going to feed, raise up to a big healthy bird, and have for Thanksgiving dinner. The idea was economical. It was cheaper to buy a baby turkey and feed it, than to buy a processed turkey in November. My brother and I were assigned to feed the baby bird and take care of its daily needs.

Daddy built the turkey coup and outfitted it for the needs of the young bird. Visitors viewed the turkey. They agreed raising your own turkey was a good idea. During all the feeding, caring for daily needs, and visiting the bird, we got rather friendly with it. We talked to it, and it made turkey sounds back. Jerry and I were not thinking of it as Thanksgiving dinner. It became a pet.

Some Thanksgiving celebrations are outstanding in memories. A lot of things come together for that outstanding Thanksgiving memory. The day before Thanksgiving came. Dad told us it was time to kill the turkey. The trauma of the statement cannot be overstated. Dad might as well said we would kill the family dog for dinner. It would have the same shock. We were devastated, in disbelief, we were expected to eat our friend.

To this day, I can't describe that Thanksgiving. It was outstanding! My brother and I didn't eat. We couldn't even eat the vegetables. We never talked about that Thanksgiving again. We never raised another turkey!

We have no turkey pictures! The little bird in the picture used here was photographed by an unknown artist and posted on the web. It looks like the baby turkey in my memories. Did the photographer raise turkeys to eat?

Our family realized we thought of animals differently. If it had life, we couldn't take it away. I still will not eat turkey. Meat is never an important part of my diet. I suppose I could be called a vegetarian.

Years passed, and we shopped in grocery stores for the little meat we ate. The day came in Home

Frances Darnell Whited

Economics class when the teacher announced each student's next assignment. We were expected to kill a chicken, strip off the feathers, cut out unusable body parts, and cook the processed chicken. I still remember the alarm going off inside me. There was no way on God's Green Earth, I, Darnell Grigsby, would do that. That's what I told my parents that evening. During this period in education history, all girls were expected to take this class. They prepared themselves for a happy marriage and home life. There seemed to be no options about killing a chicken until the day came to do it. I watched as other girls chopped the heads of the birds. Nausea and anger built inside me. I was the last girl left alone with the teacher and the chicken after school. I guess that was the day I became the school rebel, for I stated, "I'm not going to do it."

Young ladies did not rebel against their teachers. I knew I could not and would not follow these instructions. The anger of the teacher was obvious. She told me I would behead the bird. She put the ax in my hand, took my arm, and chopped off the head. I was given instructions to finish the rest of the processing. I don't remember anything after that but the nightmare of blood and feathers. I was traumatized. I knew my parents would be unhappy with me for refusing to follow class instructions. I confessed what I had done and told my side of the story at home that night. I also told my parents I was never going back in that class again. I could read recipes and buy whatever I needed in the grocery store. And besides that, I cooked for my family for years!

The next day at school I told my principal my story. I cooked since I was tall enough to reach the stove. I read a cookbook easily and knew how to buy groceries. The understanding principal, Drew Collier, assigned me to "study hall."

Mr. Collier noted my developing personality for he was prepared for my next rebellion. All girls took typing class, but I was not one of the "all girls." I didn't complete the required typing classes with the rest of my classmates. I don't remember my reasoning for dropping it. Mr. Collier's wisdom started advanced mathematics classes for a few other like-minded students. We, the misfits of Cleveland High School, excelled in mathematics: algebra, geometry and trigonometry. We fit perfectly in these classes.

Looking back on those years from turkey to chicken and the economics of life, maybe trauma and a bit of rebellion are good things. Mr. Collier told my parents they should find the money for me to go to college. Daddy argued I would only get married. It was a waste of money on a girl. Mr. Collier explained my scores on the ACT test to Daddy. Mr. Collier was a highly respected man in our town. If this was what he thought was best, my family would find a way to educate me beyond high school.

When my former principal found out I became a principal, he gave me the best counsel a new principal could have. "Never forget what your children bring with them to school. It may be the best part of their life." When I stood on the front steps of the school each morning, I looked at the faces of young people. Did they leave behind a trauma? Would I make a difference in their life as Mr. Collier made the difference for me? Would I recognize the young rebel? Was this the right education for a rebellious child?

Thomas Jefferson is quoted as saying, "A little rebellion now and then…is a medicine necessary for the sound health of government." One Thanksgiving turkey and a little rebellion helped write this story!

And by the way, we have a saying in our family, "We don't eat our friends."

My Mississippi Summer

Darnell and Budd Rainey

My first husband was Budd Rainey, a true Army brat. His mom and dad were Army officers in World War II. His dad was a veterinarian from Ohio. His mom grew up on Royal Street in New Orleans and graduated from Tulane as a nurse. Budd, their only son, didn't fit the college scene. He enlisted in the Air Force after high school graduation. Budd and I met in the summer of 1963. In the spring of 1964, after Basic Training, he was stationed at England Air Force Base in Alexandria, Louisiana. It was a troubled time in the United States with the controversial war in Vietnam and the Civil Rights Movement.

Budd and I had a brief courtship and married on April 18, 1964 before he left for Vietnam. He got a "Leave" and came home to Alabama. On Friday night, I got my hair fixed for the Saturday morning wedding. With my hair all styled, Budd picked me up from the "beauty shop" in Toad Frog Hollow. Within a few minutes, we were in a car accident on Highway 79. It totaled his car and sent me to the hospital by ambulance. With the car totaled, all our bruises and pain, the wedding proceeded as planned. We married at my family's house on Tuscaloosa Road. His grandmother did not attend because she did not approve of his marriage to a backwoods, country girl. We ate lunch at Ellis Café in Cleveland afterward with my family. We talked about the upcoming trip. My traveling experience was limited! I'd never been far from Cleveland. Mother and Daddy worried about this trip. The ignorance of my young age prevented me from doubting my ability to leave home.

Since Budd's car was demolished beyond repair, we didn't have a car to travel back to Louisiana. Budd's mother let her driver, Bobby, and his friend drive us in her car to get us back to Alexandria. Freedom Riders and what would someday be called "the Mississippi Summer" didn't cross my mind. Dad's words of wisdom as we were leaving were to drive straight to Louisiana. Only stop for gas. It never occurred to me two black men, one white man, and a white girl could be perceived as Freedom Riders headed to Mississippi. Somewhere along the way, I understood Dad's worries. We only stopped for a fast gas fill-up and brief bathroom break. "White Only" signs were real. We were met with stares, not of curiosity, but hostility. It was apparent Bobby knew the cause of the unfriendliness which met us at any stop we made. Already miserable from the car accident, we had the stress of an Alabama car tag, two black companions, and a drive south across Mississippi. We didn't eat in any cafes. Our companion's uneasiness became worse as the day went on, and we finally crossed into Louisiana. Without any problems, we made it to the little apartment in Alexandria. We said goodbye to our friend Bobby. He drove all night with minimum stops and made it safely back to Guntersville, Alabama. We would not see him again. Later, we learned blacks and whites disappeared in Mississippi doing what we did.

Unlike Budd, I was raised in an all-white Southern town. I had no contact with blacks or people from other countries. I didn't know the reality of prejudice. He traveled the world with his parents and understood intolerance. As a military "brat," he experienced unfairness first hand.

Years later, I knew "the Mississippi Summer" was the most violent time in the South since Reconstruction. I found a picture on the internet of a burning Greyhound bus. Smoke is coming out as the driver sits with his head down. An S & H Green Stamp

Anniston, Alabama, 1961

sign stands beside him.

I telephoned the Birmingham Civil Rights Institute and spoke with Mr. Wayne Coleman. He confirmed the credit for this picture is given to photographer, Joseph (Joe) Posteleone, of *The Anniston Star.* It was taken in Anniston, Alabama, in 1961.

At that point, I lived my entire life never knowing what civil rights really meant. I knew only one black person by the age of eighteen when I met Bobby. I asked myself, "How can we hate others because they are different?" I was a naive country girl with no experience in the real world.

Budd went to Vietnam and was there on our first wedding anniversary. He came back to Louisiana. He had months of strange behavior when he heard loud unexpected sounds. There was no PTSD in those days. We learned to fish the bayous and boil crayfish. He seemed to put Vietnam behind him. He never talked about that faraway country and none of our friends talked about the war.

The Civil Rights Movement continued throughout the South and on to Washington, DC. Young men continued to die in a distant country they called 'Nam.' The Vietnam veterans came back to an unfriendly homecoming. Budd never recovered from the years of military life with his troubled parents who had seen World War II. He became another troubled veteran of the war in Vietnam.

Just a Critter

In 1968, Budd and I moved from Alexandria, Louisiana, to Auburn, Alabama. I found a small house on Debardeleben Street and got a job in the Forestry Department at the university. Budd thought of becoming a veterinarian like his father, Paul Alston Rainey. But, he was not happy with the college life and only attended one semester. He went to work for Fob James at Diversified Products in Opelika. James would one day become the governor of Alabama.

We decided I would finish my college days at Auburn University. Auburn, after all, was where I always wanted to be. The university was a huge change for me, but I was back on track. I changed my major, gave up my idea of becoming a veterinarian and planned for a degree in Elementary Education.

In a year, my college track diverted again. One morning in class, I felt sick, but it went away. During an important test the following week, it happened again. I felt sick. This time, it was worse. Needless to say, it was not worry over a test. I was having a baby. The heat of June, July, August, and September was awful. I didn't enroll for fall classes. The day came, in October of 1969, when I really knew I was going to have a baby. The pain started early, with a trip to my doctor. He sent me home to wait a little longer. I phoned my Mom and Dad and told them, "Today is the day." I shopped for groceries and makeup, friends came to visit, and everyone waited for the time to go to Lee County Hospital. There is no need to go into the details of the hospital wait and the birth of my only child. We decided on his name, Bart Alston Rainey.

That day my Dad gave him the name we grew to love and often used. As the family gathered to see the first grandson, my Dad said, "Well, he is just a little critter." I told Dad, maybe a big bird. Mom was not pleased with our joking about her first grandbaby. Dad suffered more than I in the childbirth, and he was ready to leave. As he started to go, he said, "Well, Critter, I'll see you later."

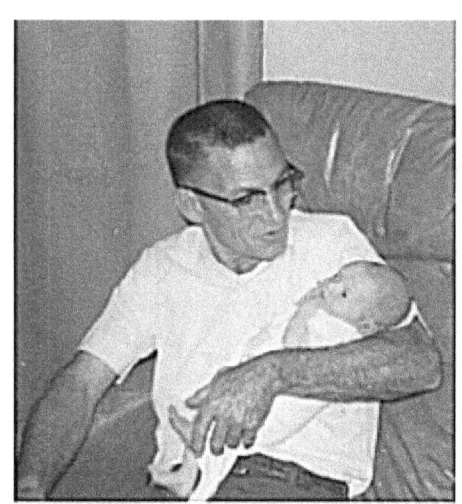

Odell Grigsby and Grandson Bart

My little "Critter" was born. Nicknames come about in strange ways. My brother, after listening to Dad, started calling him "Critter." Next, my Uncle Bud came to visit him, and he, too, used the name "Critter." Bart became known in the family as "Critter." The people who used that name are all gone now. Mom asks on occasions, "How's Critter?"

At the time, I didn't know Critter would be the only child I would have. Mother Nature and God had different plans for me. Years later, I referred to him as my miracle. We moved from Auburn when he was only three months old and settled in a little house on Ridgeway Drive in Oneonta. He had the love and support of family, life in a small town, and a safe place to grow and play. He became a free spirit. I use the term, "free spirit," with a smile. Much like his mom, he was never going to "fit" the standard school curriculum. Also, like me, his spelling and grammar caused him problems. He graduated from Oneonta City School, and I told him I felt like I graduated a second time! He tried college at Snead State, then UAB, and finally, one day he spoke with me. It was a brief conversation, "Regular college is not for me." He wanted to attend Alabama Aviation College, and that was the right "fit" for Bart. He graduated and worked at airports across the country. His major break came with his job at Gulfstream Aerospace, in Savannah, Georgia, where he worked on the prototype for the G5 aircraft. At Gulfstream, he learned the needed skills to create his own aircraft maintenance business.

Bart moved back to Alabama with his wife, Hanh, and two children, Matthew and Rachael. He became a successful business man, creating RainAir Aircraft Services with aircraft maintenance facilities at Albertville, Tuscaloosa, and Birmingham airports. He heard about aircraft all of his life from his Granddad Odell, who he called Paps. Bart spent many hours with his grandfather on Tuscaloosa Road. He played in the same woods where I

Bart "The Critter" Rainey

played as a child on Grandpa Albert's farm when my parents lived in the old house. He spent hours with his Paps. He grew up knowing his extended family because of Dad. They loaded up in Dad's old Ford pick-up truck and traveled down the dusty, back roads of Blount County.

In our modern world, it is sometimes difficult for families to spend time together. I often told Bart, "We are building memories, and you never know where you will find one."

Recently, I asked Bart for a story for my book, a memory he wanted written down on paper. This is Bart's story from childhood. "The rain this morning reminded me of spending time with Paps. We built a fire in the fireplace of the "poutin' house." We sat near the fire, talked, and listened to music. I kept the fire going, and I'd run outside to look for wood. My cousin, Anthony, and I spent a lot of time with Paps. He told old stories about growing up by the river. He told us about arrowheads in the fields. He carried us fishing at King's Bend near the old Grigsby homeplace. He liked that place best, and he had a favorite fishing hole. He fished there all his life. We sometimes fished at Swann Bridge, but he didn't like the road down to the river. He said the teenagers messed it up when they made all those mud holes with their four-wheeled drive vehicles. Paps always had a garden beside the house and grew huge tomatoes. Those tomatoes were the best I ever ate. He taught me how to grow hot peppers and make pepper sauce. He always called me 'Critter.' I miss him."

Frances Darnell Whited

A Mystery in the Picture Box

In the hundreds of old pictures belonging to my grandma and my mom, one picture stood out above all others. I showed it to Mom, and she had no idea who the people were or why they were dressed that way. Why this distasteful picture was in the picture box will remain a mystery.

One Saturday after a meeting at the Oneonta Public Library, I noticed Steve Smith's antique store across the street was open. I turned the car around and stopped for a visit. I knew Steve's father many years ago when he owned antiques in a corner store downtown.

I roamed around for a while talking about different items, reminiscing about old times, when the aging picture came to mind. I

Still a Mystery

described this old, worn photograph with men dressed as women. I told him they held black-faced dolls. He had an answer, maybe not the one I wanted, but it sent me toward my research.

In 1848, Blackface Minstrel Shows were an American pastime. This form of performance was also popular in Britain. Think of Stephen Foster, the American composer, and his type of songs, many written for traveling minstrels. Traveling minstrel shows reached the pinnacle of their popularity between 1850 and 1870. With a computer search, there's more to read on this "bizarre art form" in the *Encyclopedia of Appalachia*.

With this said, I put the mystery of the picture to rest. I will probably never know how it came to be in Granny Anna's picture box.

Frances Darnell Whited

Vittles, Fiddles, and Bluegrass in the Front Yard

In the warm Alabama weather of my childhood, I knew there would be Bluegrass in the front yard. I'm talking about musicians with instruments playing the old country music. It happened on Saturday after lunch. People came over to play. It was a spontaneous event, passed on by word of mouth with not much formal invitation. Chairs appeared, and the musicians with their instruments came wandering up. They never set up in the backyard. The front yard was a tradition. I don't know how many years the event went on, when it started, or when it ended. I remember there were no female musicians, just an assortment of men dressed in their Saturday clothes. Some wore hats, others had caps, and a few were bareheaded.

During those days, I wasn't a fan of 'tuning and picking.' The men had to figure out who would sit where, decide on the first song, and then, tune up the instruments. It seemed to me it took forever for everyone to get tuned up for just one song. The song ended and discussion about what to play next would start. They finally decided and tuned up again and on and on. By the third song, I began to ease away from the front yard to go about my own business. When Daddy wasn't around, I listened to a new music of which he did not approve. He let me know his dislike. I was taught to play the piano and could read notes. I played reasonably well but not with enthusiasm. On the other hand, my brother learned by hearing the sounds in the front yard. As a young fellow, he watched and listened. One day, he played the banjo and guitar with enthusiasm and started a band named the "Invaders."

Bluegrass in Blount County also meant knowing the Sawyer Mountain Boys. The group was made of J.D. Whited, Ralph Whited, and Carter Whited. They were living legends, a history of the Bluegrass of old Blount County and the South. I was fortunate to know and hear them play. The song they are best known for is "Possum up a Gum Stump." Ralph never married. He lived with his bachelor brother, Brady, in the house inherited from their prosperous grandfather. The old house on Highway 231 was a gathering place for real Bluegrass music. In 1988, a **Southern Democrat** writer, Sue Tidwell, did a wonderful article about the Whited Boys.

Joyce Cauthen is credited as project director for an album of Whited music. Ralph Whited has a website dedicated to him. "Possum up a Gum Stump" has been preserved for future generations.

(Photograph courtesy of the Blount County Memorial Museum)
Selmer Joe Taylor, J. D., Ralph, and Carter Whited

Bluegrass music sometimes brought with it homemade ice cream. Ice cream freezers showed up like the musicians. Ice and ice cream salt were added. Everyone took turns at turning the handle. We learned where to station the freezers because the salt water killed Daddy's grass. He hated those big brown spots of dead grass! Some days there was food outside on tables, so we had 'vittles and fiddles.' Looking back, I wish I remembered the names of all the musicians who played and ate at our house on Tuscaloosa Road.

By accident, I heard a band at the 14th Annual Bloom-N-Pie days near Blountsville. I listened for a while. I mentioned my childhood days with Bluegrass in the front yard in Cleveland. An older musician said, "I remember those days in Odell's front yard." The man, Mr. Pate, played music with the assortment of men who showed up on Saturday.

That day there were bales of straw under the shade trees, so I sat back down and listened to another old song. The smell of straw and food was a

Frances Darnell Whited

nice blend. The musicians talked about the next song and tuned up. My memories go back to Tuscaloosa Road on another warm Saturday evening.

Oil Mops, Radiators, and Cleveland School

There is a place on a little space of land called Cleveland School. I read in the **Heritage of Blount County**, "The Confederate census tells us Sarah Beavers was teaching school there before 1862. In 1905, the school moved to its present location." There were many changes on the site, and I was part of one change. "The aging white building erected in 1925 was replaced in 1963." That was the year of my graduation.

Most girls took typing and home economics. Some dropped out before graduation to marry and have children. I remember the library and the quietness of what was called "study hall." Mr. Collier was seen with an oil mop going down the hallways. The building smelled of oil. In the winter, we were never really too warm. To get warm, you stood as close as was safe to the hot radiators. I remember the feel of the burns on the back of my legs.

School days in Cleveland, Alabama

There were four people who influenced my school life: Miss Bonnie Ridgeway, Hugh O'Shields, Ruby O'Shields, and Mr. Drew Collier. When I think of them now, I wish all children had these role models. They made a positive difference in my future.

In elementary school, Miss Ridgeway was the first. It may be my rebellious nature started back then. Another student of this dear lady remembered I took his bright red apple. Being the Southern lady I proclaim to be, I said, "Well, I'll be. Surely not, there must have been a reason." He said he regretted getting me in trouble.

Coach Hugh O'Shields was another influence in my days at Cleveland. He lived with Annie Ruth and Sidney Bellenger when he first moved to Cleveland as a single young man. Annie Ruth was Mom's first cousin.

My parents made an arrangement with Coach to pick us up in the morning for school. We wouldn't take the long walk to the bus stop in the cold or rain. The rules for the ride were simple: be polite and on time. Coach had a lot of patience with my little brother, Jerry, when he started the first grade. But, we lost our ride because of Jerry's morning temper tantrums and crying spells.

Coach's wife, Ruby, made a strong impact on my thinking, as she taught us to look into the future. She told our class one day about the possibilities ahead of us. We would fly in airplanes. There would be movies in our homes. She was a reader of all kinds of literature and shared with her classes. On my first airplane flight, I thought of her. Later, my first job at Oneonta City School was teaching seventh and eighth grade math. Mrs. O'Shields became my boss. She was the principal of the high school.

Drew Collier was the greatest influence on my life. He guided many of us down a path to success and taught us to take the road less traveled. As our high school principal, he saw the rebels in a few of us. We didn't fit. He saw the need for a change in the old curriculum. Mr. Collier started mathematics classes for those who needed a change. While I made "C" or unsatisfactory in English, I flew high with A's and flourished in the algebra, geometry, trigonometry, and calculus. He talked with me about my ACT scores when I scored second year college on the test. He sent me to meet with a team for summer work at Redstone Arsenal. I was the only girl in a room full of boys who interviewed that day. I was voted "Best Dressed" in my yearbook but took little home economics. Mr. Collier gave me the dream of an educated future.

Great friendships formed in high school. Wilma Barbee moved to Cleveland and lived with Peggy Hunt in the Tracy Brown House on Highway 231. This house fascinated me all my life, and Wilma lived there. We walked up the staircase to the bedrooms. It was like being in the movie "Gone with the Wind." On weekends, we rolled up our blue jeans, talked about rock and roll, and walked to town. At Pass's store, with less than a quarter, we brought a coke and a candy bar and strolled back down the dusty road to my home. Tootle (Beatrice Bullard) talked of Elvis Presley, and Dianna Johnson spent the night with me because I had no older brothers. Annette Sloan and I "double dated" with boys we thought we'd marry. Jim Allen, Jerry Cornelius, and Wilford Shelton disappeared from my life. We all went our separate ways the day after high school graduation, thinking life would never change. It did change. Years passed before we began to come back together with high school reunions.

I think of the journey from Cleveland High School, to Louisiana, to Auburn, and back to Blount County. There were a lot of roads not taken on my journey to these pages. Today, I read again Robert Frost's poem about the road not taken. Back then, I didn't know the difference one road, one turn, could make in life.

Frances Darnell Whited

Loafing and Cherry Vanilla Ice Cream

My daddy used the word "loafing" when the family loaded up in our best car for a trip around Blount County. The word "loafing" has a special meaning for me. It means "aimless wandering, idling one's time away." Loafing usually happened after lunch on Saturday or after church on Sunday. It didn't require much preparation. Dad gassed up the car. We might visit family, or go find something or someplace Mom or Dad heard about and wanted to see. We put on our best shoes, made sure we were clean, and wore freshly cleaned clothes.

My favorite loafing was going for an ice cream cone on Saturday evening. Cherry vanilla ice cream was a new flavor in my childhood. There was a grocery store, and I believe it was called Odis and Robin's, or Helen's. It was on the right on Highway 231 before we got to Oneonta. Daddy heard they sold this new delicious treat. We loaded up and loafed our way down Tuscaloosa Road to the highway, heading to the grocery store. It was a special day because my little brother and I got two scoops in the crusty cone. Cherry vanilla in those days had huge red, sweet cherries, not pieces, and the most wonderful smell. If the weather was hot, we ate quickly because the car had no air-conditioning. A creamy stream oozed down the side of the cone before we knew it. Mom would say, "Lick it, lick it! Don't make a mess in the car! And don't bite the bottom out!" All the way back to Tuscaloosa Road, we licked the melting, sweet liquid. We were two happy kids in the back seat of an old car loafing on an Alabama evening.

Grigsby Home on the Old Tuscaloosa Road ca 1955

There is a picture of our house in Cleveland with two cars in the front yard. Daddy claimed the white one because he drove to Birmingham for work. A friend told me this car looked like a Ford Fairlane, but he wasn't sure about the year. The other car was Mom's vehicle, maybe a 1947 Ford Super Deluxe with four doors. She drove it around Blount County. I remember the doors opened in the middle, to the left and right, hinged differently from today's cars. We sat on the running board and ate when we went to the cotton fields. I asked the question, "Did this car have what was called 'suicide doors'?" Some folks referred to them as "coach doors." It was all the same and caused some safety concerns but back to the loafing.

A friend used "loaf" recently in an e-mail. He was going to loaf away the day while I struggled for words for my stories. It had been years since I heard it used. It made me happy to read the word. Memories of those long ago days came back with the simple pleasure of going for a ride, just loafing away the evening. I looked the word up online, to find out more about its origin. I wish I hadn't done that! In this modern world, the simple word has changed. I question whether for the better. Today, we have several types of loafing: urban, social, creative, and of all things, cyber loafing!

Ok, folks, it's Saturday evening. Let's go loafing…oh, do we want to go urban loafing, social loafing, creative loafing, or cyber loafing? I think someone went a bit too far with the simple pleasure. My friends and I will continue to loaf the back roads of Blount County, maybe find a grocery store, or a café, that sells cherry vanilla ice cream. We'll get lots of paper napkins, turn the air-conditioning down low, and lick slowly.

Frances Darnell Whited

Postal Progress and Conversations with Edwina Bryan

Eldridge Bynum wrote his story of Cleveland, Alabama, in a 1989 book called *Cleveland, Alabama 35049*. As I read his stories, many of my memories of Cleveland came back to me. Some of my outstanding memories were my trips from Cleveland to Oneonta on a mail truck. My mail truck experiences settled to the back of mind until I met Edwina Bryan at the Magnolia House, an assisted living home. Both my mother and brother lived there, so I visited often. Edwina knew me all my life, and I enjoyed listening to her tales of Cleveland.

Edwina Bryan, Postmistress

An opportunity came for me to sit with her and listen to her stories. She was the Postmistress of the Cleveland Post Office, officially appointed January 20, 1973. Before her, Virgil Head was the Postmaster of my early childhood. After one conversation about the early days of the town, I was ready to learn more from her. Before leaving that day, I sat on the front porch in the sunshine and talked with my brother about the things she told me. He looked at the old pictures I copied from the museum. It was a good day. I phoned my son to tell him about my visit with Edwina and how well Jerry was doing.

Unfortunately, the next morning after that talk, the first love in my life, my brown-eyed brother, became sick again and died the following morning. He lost his lifelong battle with schizophrenia. We organized his funeral, got pictures for his video, and selected his favorite kind of music for the service. After the funeral, I could not look at pictures of my dead ancestors. I couldn't find any words for stories. I put all my notes in files. Edwina's conversation became lost in my grief. I boxed up all the pictures from the past and put them in my closet. The last ten years of my life was organized around helping with Jerry's declining health. There were weeks of nightmares about his death. There were final things to take care of and hospital bills. A day came when I realized a part of my life was over. There was no going back to the white rockers to talk with him. I'd never hear him play the guitar or banjo again. I found it difficult to walk into the Magnolia House to visit Mom. I spoke briefly to the staff and residents. In late January, I sat for a short time with Edwina. It was late February before I looked at the notes for the story. My notes and thoughts waited for me to come back. In late July, Edwina's story began.

Edwina was born in 1930, at her parents' home in Cleveland. Her parents were Edwin and Ethel (Rutherford) Pass. Her story goes like this. Her relatives left Georgia during the time of the Civil War, when the guns got too close, with Union soldiers nearing them. They packed all they carried in a wagon. They traveled a worn road from Georgia and settled in the area we know as Cleveland. There were a lot of round rocks in the fields which were removed before the family could begin farming. They piled them out of the way. Those old "round rocks were put on a flat house" where Edwina's grandson, Bobby Baker, now lives. Edwina recalled a heading mill, which fired twenty-four hours a day. Her daddy worked there at night and farmed during the day. She remembered her Granddaddy Rutherford used his own money to build a telephone line from Devertown, near Moss Bridge, to Doctor Brown's office in Cleveland for emergency calls.

Edwina told of her daddy selling milk to the convict camp. She went with him to deliver the milk, and the black cook always had a special treat for her. Her daddy asked this man if he would come to work for him when he got out of prison. The story continues this fellow killed a man in South Alabama. Mr. Edwin asked him why he killed the man. The honest reply was, "I didn't kill him. I shot him, and he died." Even knowing this, Mr. Edwin felt comfortable giving him a job. On the day the fellow was released, he disappeared from Cleveland. Some weeks later, he returned to Blount County and the job. He went to South Alabama to see his people one last time.

We came back to the conversation about the post office. The mail truck I remembered became the subject of discussion. I rode in the back of the covered truck many times along with other folks. We didn't talk, just sat there, as the road passed under the truck. There was no heat in winter and no air-conditioning in summer. Not everyone owned a car back then. The mail truck turned into a cheap way to get across the county. We believe it only cost twenty-five cents round trip. The truck started its daily route around 7:30 each morning from Garden City where the mail came in by train. The driver traveled from there to Blountsville, then Cleveland, and on to Oneonta. If you went back home on the mail truck, it left promptly at 11:30 a.m. from Oneonta. You better be loaded and get ready because the mail truck always left on time.

In the early days of the post office, it was located in the center of downtown Cleveland. A sidewalk passed down the street in front of the stores and on to its central location, an outhouse found behind the buildings. Edwina reminded me "in those days," there wasn't a lot a choice about what to buy in the local stores. And with a serious look she said, "You had everything you needed to eat because you grew it on the farm. You raised hogs and seasoned everything with lard." My memories are pretty much the same, because we grew most of what we ate. Mom canned, we cooked with lard, and we saved used grease.

In Granny Anna's picture boxes, I found many unused post cards and lots of empty, stamped envelopes. They are an interesting documentation of the changes in postal prices, services, and the importance of the United States Post Office from the past. If you wanted stamps or cards, you left a note in the box with your money. If you wanted a ride to town, you waited by the mailbox. Things have definitely changed.

Talk of Tuscaloosa Road

For months, I thought about a visit to talk with a long time resident of Cleveland. I heard of Jesse Davis for years, and he is a brother-in-law of my friend and classmate, Jerry Cornelius. Many times, I talked about Tuscaloosa Road to Jerry and also about our Cornelius connection. He mentioned Jesse's years with Alabama Power, and Jesse knew a lot about the old roads and the old families of Blount County. The idea he might add to my knowledge of Tuscaloosa Road stayed in the corners of my mind as I occupied myself with other stories. On a trip to take pictures in Cleveland, I drove past Jesse's house, and I knew it was time to follow up on what he might add to my history of Tuscaloosa Road.

Camp Cleveland, a State Convict Camp ca 1930 - 1950

On the day of the visit, I sat on the sofa and listened to Jesse talk about his Cleveland memories. Jesse was born in 1933, and he saw many changes come to Cleveland. Our conversation rambled in and out, and all about, like an old stagecoach road, but it had a destination. I explained I was searching for Tuscaloosa Road, and smiling, he began to tell me about his memories.

Jesse's story begins: "I remember the paving of Highway 231 when I was a boy. I could watch from a cotton field. There was a convict camp on Tuscaloosa Road below Charles Johnson's daddy's house. You know, Charles and Villa were my classmates, so I remember where Charles grew

---

[3] Photograph of Camp Cleveland courtesy of the Blount County Memorial Museum.

up. The convicts worked the road out there in front of where this house is now. They used six mules to pull a skid. You know, they didn't have bulldozers in those days. The convicts built the culverts out of big rocks. The rocks aren't there anymore. They were big culverts. I think the cows could cross under the road to the other side. If a convict tried to escape, they used bloodhounds to track them. Sometimes, Mr. Tidwell, who trained the hounds, would let the people around Cleveland know the day he was training the dogs. You could hear the hounds howling in the fields around Cleveland. I was in a hunting club in South Alabama. One day, I started talking to an old gentleman who lived down there. He asked me where I was from, and I told him Cleveland in Blount County. The old gentleman laughed, and then said 'I know the town. I served time up there.' He had been in the camp."

With a few words, I redirected the conversation back to the road. I told Jesse about seeing glimpses of an old roadbed near Dry Creek and Green's Chapel Church. Jesse began, "That's old Tuscaloosa Road. My uncle used to drive up from Inglenook to get us kids on a Saturday or Sunday. There would be seven or eight of us packed in the car and the rumble seat and hanging on the running boards. We'd drive down that old road. It's near Ricky Gilliland's house. One day, the old bridge washed away when the water got high. When you got time, one day I can show you where the road was. It went on down below the Gilliland place to the Tadlock place. You can still see parts of it in the woods."

Our conversation lasted about an hour that day. Jesse, like many of us, learned to recognize the landmarks of our county. One thought I had, as I closed the door to Jesse's house, was "One day, I will make time to drive Jesse around Cleveland looking for Tuscaloosa Road."

My search for a map I can touch with the name Old Tuscaloosa Road on it may go on after I finish my last story. These stories live on in the pages. Who knows? Maybe, someone else will take the torch and look for the old road, my Old Tuscaloosa Road.

Memories of Phenix City

When we think back on our lives, there are often events which shake our belief in humanity and goodness of the world. On my ninth birthday, June of 1954, I experienced such an event. This occurrence became significant across our state of Alabama. It was written about in newspapers, talked about on radio, and became part of Alabama history.

That June, Mom, Dad, Jerry and I loaded the best car for a trip to Winter Haven, Florida. My Aunt Villa and her two girls moved there after Uncle Charles died. In those days, there were no interstates to make the long trip faster and easier. School was out for the summer, so it was an ideal time to visit them. The car had no air-conditioning, and the little side windows were turned inward to give us a blast of hot air. Jerry and I often suffered from car sickness on long trips, and the heat of summer only added to our misery on the long trip.

By the time we reached Phenix City, Alabama, Jerry began to show signs of car sickness. It was something that happened. Dramamine, the miracle drug for this, could not be bought over the counter. Dad said, "We gotta find a doctor!" He talked with Mom about what they were going to do. She would stay in the locked car with us while he talked with the man at a service station. We waited in the hot car for Daddy to come back. He got directions to a doctor in Phenix City. Everyone stayed in the car while Daddy went upstairs to the doctor's office. Leaving us in a hurry, Daddy said, "We need to get out of here before the sun goes down." Dad was often dramatic!

I was young and miserable from the hot travel, but I knew something wasn't quite right. We were looking for a doctor in Phenix City, Alabama. That day, the town of Phenix City was unimportant to me. Daddy found the doctor and got the prescription he needed. I remember the talk of getting the prescription filled as quickly as possible. Maybe, I thought all the hurry was to get the medicine in Jerry before he started to vomit. I don't remember anything about leaving Phenix City, except both Mom and Dad seemed relieved. We made it to Winter Haven. Then, I realized the rush to leave Phenix City. Adults talked about stopping in that town for medicine. It seemed everyone knew the tales of crime in the Alabama city. Albert Patterson was elected Attorney General for the State of Alabama. People of the state knew Patterson's goal planned to clean up "Sin City."

Bad news is a powerful thing, especially when it happens on your ninth birthday. The stop on our last trip to Florida was fresh in my memories when I heard the news. I remembered again Daddy being cautious. I walked into the kitchen and heard Mom and Dad's conversation about the murder of Albert Patterson. He was killed on June 18, my birthday.

Years later, Dad loaded up the family to go to the theater to watch a movie. It was called "The Phenix City Story." I remember the violence portrayed in the black and white film. One vivid scene showed the body of a young black girl, murdered, and tossed out on a street. We watched the movie unfold with the Alabama Democratic Party declaring Patterson won the election for State Attorney General. Patterson, declared a winner on June 10, 1954, but he never served in that office. The murder of Albert Patterson on June 18, 1954, was forever carved deep in memories.

I have often thought about that day and heard a lot about "Sin City." When the memories of this tragedy came back this year, I decided to read again about that period in Alabama history. I ordered the book, *The Tragedy and the Triumph of Phenix City, Alabama*. Margaret Anne Barnes's words filled my thoughts as I read her book and looked at the picture[4]. I felt the anger of the young Darnell. Mr. Patterson was killed on her special day.

In Montgomery, a marble statue of Albert Patterson stands on the north side of Alabama's State Capitol. The date of 18 June 1954 is carved beneath his lame left foot. He is supported by his cane. While I was President of Alabama Instructional Media Association, I was in Montgomery a lot. On a spring day, I visited the statue of the man who made such a strong impact on my childhood memories. The day he died made his death personal to me, and I felt as if I knew him. I said goodbye to a man I never knew but often thought about June 18th.

---

[4] This photograph is reproduced from Margaret Anne Barnes' book.

Albert Patterson

Frances Darnell Whited

An Old Country Church

After my family left Fowler Springs Baptist Church, we started attending the Cleveland Baptist Church on Highway 231. It was only about three city blocks from our house on Tuscaloosa Road. We walked the unpaved road for church services if we didn't have transportation. After a big revival, I joined the Baptist faith, baptized in the church baptistery, a large tank of unheated water. I carried an unreasonable fear of being submerged in water, so this was a true test of faith. When I became fairly good at playing the piano, I sometimes played at the church on Sunday. I did not enjoy this because I developed a case of stage fright after the first song. All things said, Cleveland Baptist Church was my church, the church of my childhood memories. My Roberts family were charter members.

One day, Mom phoned and told me they were establishing a new Baptist Church in Cleveland. I'm sure I asked, "And who are *they*?" As we know, even in church, people disagree about what is right and what is not, what should be and what should not be. After all, isn't this the reason we have so many different churches and denominations? It is not for me to say the reason for the "falling out," but another Baptist church soon started.

On January 12, 1969, at eleven o'clock, a group of twenty-two people met at the vacant house of the late Albert and Anna Johnson on Tuscaloosa Road. The purpose of the meeting was to discuss organizing a new Baptist Church in Cleveland, Alabama. Mother stated after prayer and singing, the group organized a Sunday school and agreed to meet in the Johnson house until a church was fully organized. The first pastor was Hugo Kretzschmar. The names submitted as charter members were: Martha Grigsby, Odell Grigsby, Annie Ruth Bellenger, Sidney Bellenger, Lelila Nash, Evelyn Copeland, Virgil Copeland, Gertrude Hudson, Louise Blackwood, Coy Blackwood, Connie Blackwood, Ann Hill, Lena Patterson, Hubert Patterson, Mabel Kretzschmar, and Hugo Kretzschmar.

This newly established church was known as Westside Baptist Church. Land for the church was property which years before belonged to Isaac Roberts of Tuscaloosa Road. My brother and I played in the woods and fields Isaac owned. These fields and woods were replaced with the church built on Highway 79 in Cleveland.

Years later, near the end of the Tuscaloosa Road, the Baptist members who didn't change to Westside Baptist Church, built a modern church. They left the building of my childhood. I have a picture of the "old" Cleveland Baptist Church on Highway 231. Anytime I drive the route north, I see the aging building. I think of the hymns we sang, and the time I was submerged in that cold water. I didn't question whose religion was correct. I was just a Baptist, who attended the brick church on Highway 231 in Cleveland, Alabama.

Old Baptist Church in Cleveland, Alabama

Frances Darnell Whited

Boyd's Music Store and the Sounds of Life

Each of us has songs which touched our lives and moved our spirits to a higher place. After writing about radio and Bluegrass in the front yard, I spent some time listening to old songs which have influenced my thoughts, even helped me work past some bad days. There were many. As I edited my typing, I found their inspiration give me words I hadn't realized. Surrounding myself with books and songs, I wonder which words are mine. Words are words, I think. They belong to all of us. It's how we use them that's important.

On a sunny day, I visited the Oneonta Public Library. I searched one

The W C Boyd Music Company

more time for a map, any map that would reference the Old Tuscaloosa Road. The staff was patient and tried to help but still no map. I sat down on the floor, surrounded by old books, and breathed in that smell of aging pages. One book caught my attention, ***County Roads, A Journey through Rustic Alabama*** [5] by Carolynne Blackwell Scott. I didn't find my map, but I found a wonderful story about Boyd's Store and W.O. Boyd. I traveled back in childhood to the Oneonta store.

---

[5] Photograph of Mr. Boyd and his store taken from Carolynne Blackwell Scott's book.

Music, and the sounds of life, put to notes and words, has always been a part of my life. I don't remember knowing W. O. Boyd. I remember Boyd's Music Shop. As children, my brother and I visited many times. The sidewalk was all broken up from tree roots coming to the surface. There were overhanging limbs in front of the store. It was a magical walk into the building. We saw guitars, guitar strings, and harmonicas. Daddy bought his harmonica at Boyd's. When I learned to play the piano, I bought sheet music there. The notes and words to "How Great Thou Art" were played and sung over and over from the sheet music purchased at Boyd's. Records were ordered there and picked up later. The adults had conversations which didn't include us. We knew children were to be seen, not heard. We wandered about looking up and all around at the objects filling Boyd's Music Shop. It overflowed with mysterious things. It was like a museum of country life and items associated with music.

Later in life, my brother played beautiful songs with Glenna Boyd. Glenna and Jerry played and sung at my wedding at Palisades Park. She left our life for many years only to show up to play music at the Magnolia House. I got to see the two of them tune up, play again, and hear Glenna sing. At Christmas, local musicians like Glenna, Jackie Manes, Bob Bentley, and Tom Prickett came to play for the residents. I watched

Jerry Grigsby and Glenna Boyd at Darnell's Wedding

with tears in my eyes as I saw my brother play with them. For a brief moment in time, his schizophrenia left us all. Glenna's voice flowed down the halls of the building. By request from the residents, Jerry always played and sang one solo, his favorite song, "King of the Road." The Christmas of 2015 was the last time they played together. Jerry died the following

Frances Darnell Whited

year. Glenna's grandson died the same week, so she couldn't sing at Jerry's funeral. There was no music that year at the Magnolia House.

Music was lost to me the day my brother died. It slowly comes back, a word, a phrase, notes on the wind. Where would we be without music and the sounds of life that music makes?

Thundercloud and the Story I Could Not Write

When sixty-seven years of one's life are spent calling someone "my little brother," it's hard to give up. It's even harder to give up the need to care for that person. From the time Jerry Lynn Grigsby was born, he was the first love of my life, my little brother. Mom started me out with the phrase, "Now, take care of your little brother." We had good times in the fields of the Roberts's property. We knew who we were, and we knew our family had been part of Cleveland for a long time. What we didn't know was the future, and how fast the future came.

Someday, I will write the story, maybe a book, about our family's journey with Jerry, our "Thundercloud," but that will have to wait. It's too soon. He died December 1, 2016. There were awful times when I couldn't make sense of his world. There were days filled with anger because I couldn't share with anyone. I never reached out for counseling for myself. I put it away in a dark abyss. I spent a lifetime missing my little brother.

"Thundercloud"

There was a lifetime of goodbyes to things we might have shared, but the disease took them away.

Jerry was diagnosed with schizophrenia in his early twenties. Someday, I'll write about the journey he took from an amazing little brown-eyed boy to the tormented aging man. I'll write about the joy he found in music and the wonderful talent for stringed instruments. There will be words about hospitals, disrespect for the mentally ill, and the lack of doctors who listen and communicate with family. I'll mention the nursing homes that would not accept a schizophrenic. There will also be a "thank you" to those who understood, cared, and stood by him all those years. Each day, good memories flow up from the darkness and bring me a smile.

A few days before he died, he told me in vivid details what he called the "Levels of the Gods." We were on our way to another hospital. Things were not right. We talked about American Indian flute music and the calming nature of a flute. I never told him we were not Native American. It would only confuse him or made him argue the point. As children, Jerry and I learned about old healing ways, signs from the unknown, and a respect for nature.

On a sunny evening, we sat in rocking chairs on the porch of the Magnolia House and talked about my pictures of old Cleveland. I told him about the book I planned to write. We talked about Edwina's stories. Leaving the parking lot that day, I phoned my son as I often did to tell him about "Unk" (Uncle). It was the best day I could remember, and he seemed so normal. The call that came the next morning was unreasonable, what could be wrong? In less than twenty hours, his life was over. The news spread fast around our little hometown Jerry, Thundercloud, died.

For my little brother, funeral traditions were put aside. The Cleveland Funeral home is located at the end of Old Tuscaloosa, near the site of old Camp Cleveland. They knew our family. They knew Jerry would not want Baptist hymns. That was fine with them. The building was full on December 3, 2016, and standing around the pews, more folks stood without seats. They came to say goodbye to Thundercloud, my little brother. We heard the music "Somewhere Over the Rainbow," by singer Israel Kamakawiwo, and I thought of bluebirds flying happy and free from troubles. We listened to "A Time and Place for Everything" based on the verse from Ecclesiastes. I know there is a time to be born and a time to die. The last song we heard was "When I Get Where I'm Going" by Brad Paisley. Maybe, Jerry is still playing.

Jerry Grigsby

My son and I drove quietly to my house on the hill after making all the preparations for his funeral. Looking down my walking trail, we saw a mother deer and her fawn. She stood for a long time looking at us as we sat in the car. She turned, walked calmly down the trail, and out of sight. We didn't say anything as we stepped out of the car. From up above, we heard the loud cry of a hawk. It flew down low over us and disappeared. At the same time, my son and I both knew we believed in signs like our ancestors of long ago. We smiled, and said at the same time, "Unk", the word we used for "Uncle."

On the day Jerry's tombstone was set in place at Westside Baptist Church Cemetery, the word spread around Cleveland, "Thundercloud's getting his marker." On it is carved, "Rest in peace, Thundercloud."

Frances Darnell Whited

Mental Health and Bryce Hospital

A family member diagnosed with mental health issues is often an embarrassment for that family. It's not talked about in polite company. Most families have someone with a mental health problem. Somewhere in the past, there may be one or two, or maybe more, ancestors with mental health issues. Maybe, they were patients at Bryce Hospital.

Bryce Hospital, in Tuscaloosa, Alabama, opened in 1861. According to my findings, it was first called the Alabama State Hospital for the Insane. There is no way for me to define what the word "insane" encompassed in those days. Years later, the hospital was renamed for Peter Bryce, a psychiatric pioneer. I was in my twenties when I first made contact with Bryce Hospital and my brother's diagnosis. The columns of white Italianate style exterior of that grand three-story building were what I first saw as we drove through the gates. Picture every horror movie you've seen about insane asylums. The visions of shackles, straitjackets, and bizarre treatments are usually the first things to come to mind. That's what happened to me that day. My fear for my brother was so great, I opened the car door, jumped out, and threw up.

Bryce Hospital, Tuscaloosa, Alabama

As my research carried me deeper into the past, I found Bryce Hospital crossed my path again and again. In the past, I clipped pictures and articles of the hospital for a file. On a visit to see my brother, I took my own photograph. I looked at my picture of the driveway and white building. The cracks in the driveway, running in different directions, stand out to me. They are symbolic of the cracks which came in our family life, the cracks in Jerry's health, and the paths of Jerry's journey. All of my life I was told to "take care of your little brother," often taking his hand as we did things together. I released my care of him to strangers at the end of that cracked driveway.

One day while visiting, I made the comment to an attendant about Jerry being "my little brother." Even when he weighed over 200 pounds, I still introduced him as "Jerry, my little brother." Jerry and I talked about that as we sat in the visiting area. I told him it was time I simply said, "my brother." He laughed, and smiling said, "It's about time."

Some doors must be closed to open new ones. I made many trips to the hospital during the years of Jerry's illness. I traveled the long drive to Tuscaloosa one more time before the old hospital was closed forever. Many changes were coming. I wanted to walk in the cemetery of the unnamed graves. My great-great-grandfather wasn't buried in the Blackwood Cemetery with his family. One of the lost graves belonged to him, Andrew Allred. He died in Bryce Hospital on September 8, 1907. I asked myself if he died alone in Bryce Hospital. He is one of the many lost names on the markers that have lost their numbers. There is shame in that period of mental health care, shame in the disrespect for the life and death of those patients in unmarked graves. Has there been enough progress made in the care and treatment of the mentally ill? Has the shame associated with being mentally ill gone away?

Jerry and Puppy

The picture of Jerry Grigsby, a little boy on Tuscaloosa Road, reflects a happy child in his overalls with a puppy. I see his bare feet. We never thought about Bryce Hospital back then. We never knew the disrespect and prejudice directed at the mentally ill.

Another Piece of Old Tuscaloosa Road

Blountsville Historical Society receives a lot of recognition for the historical park located outside the town of Blountsville on Highway 231, north. While writing about my family, I searched many, many websites looking for the mysterious Old Tuscaloosa Road. One day, a search bought me to the *AFC Cooperative Farming News.* So, I took time to read about "Bringing History to Life."

Blountsville was the county seat of Blount County back in 1819. I continued to read the old Blountsville courthouse was later used as the building that housed Blount College. Unfortunately, it burned January 5, 1895. As I read, a wonderful bit of information came to my attention, "As more and more settlers came, they traveled what became known as the Tuscaloosa-Huntsville Road and a part of the road is now the back driveway to the Blountsville Historical Park! What is now known as the Freeman House was built facing that old road around 1830. Jane Wright remembers living in that house more than a century later when she was five or six years old, having to utilize an outdoor toilet and with her mother cooking their meals on a wood-fired cook stove."

That day, I found the names of Betty Alexander and Jane Wright, two wonderful Southern ladies, happy to talk with me about my old road. They extended an invitation to me to attend the Blountsville Historical Society Christmas meeting at the old Freeman House. I told Jane about my desire to find more documentation about Tuscaloosa Road, expressing I didn't need Huntsville Road. I wanted to see the words "Old Tuscaloosa Road." Jane's reply was like a Christmas gift, "I can do that. I have it on a deed." Words could not express my excitement.

On the night of December 11, 2017, I drove from my little house on the hill to Cleveland, crossed the bridge on Highway 231, and headed on to Blountsville. In downtown Blountsville, I passed the old building that was the theater of my youth. The members welcomed me, and we shared a Christmas get-together. After the meal, Jane gave me the papers I patiently waited to read. As we talked, Jane said there used to be an old tale stating "the travelers on the road were like the Children of Israel leaving Egypt. They were excited about their journey, but there was a good bit of cussin."

In the back of the room, I sat with the old deeds. There it was in the descriptions, Old Tuscaloosa Road, shown separately from Huntsville Road. To be honest, I wanted to leave and head back home with my latest treasure, but I stayed for the meeting. When saying goodbye to the group, I don't think they realized how important the night had been to me. Coming into the historical park, I drove my car down another piece of my old road, in back of the Freeman House.

Traveling back home, my stories seemed more alive and had a deeper meaning by adding one more piece of this road. As I came to Cleveland, I turned and drove down the road of my childhood. As a little girl, didn't know the role it played in my life.

Freeman House

```
                                    DATED Aug. 3, 1965
              TO                    FILED Sept. 2, 1965
                                    ....MTG......... BOOK NO. 331  PAGE.
   The Bank of Blountsville         $7,329.00 ...... DUE Feb. 28, 1966
   Blountsville, Alabama
                       LAND IF DESCRIBED
```

The SW¼ of the SW¼ ; that part of the NW¼ of SE¼ South of Lane Fence; the SW¼ less and except 5 acres, more or less, in the SW¼ of SW¼, commencing a beech tree NE of spring about 2 rods; thence South to section line; the W to SW corner; thence due N to the Huntsbille Public Road; thence E with road to the beginning corner; Also, all that part of the NW¼ and the NW¼ NE¼ lying NW of U. S. Highway #231, all in Section 5;
The SW¼ of the SW¼, the SE¼ of SW¼, and a part of the SW¼ of SE¼ describe follows: Beginning at the SW corner of said 40, run thence E to the old Tuscaloosa Road, run thence along said road in a Northeasterly direction the point where the Old Tuscaloosa Road crosses U.S. Highway #231, run th in a Northwesterly direction along Lee Scott line to the N line of said 4 thence W to the NW corner, thence S to the point of beginning, all in Sec 32.
Also, the NE¼ of the SE¼ and all that portion of the SE¼ of SE¼ lying N of said Old Tuscaloosa Rod except 5 acres being in the NE¼ of SE¼ and SE¼ of SE¼, more particularly desobibed as follows, viz: Commencing at the Huntsville Road and running N to the Creek with the original line; thence said creek to a red elm at the upper end of fish hole, thence NW to a rock thence South to a certain stake on ~~Old Tuscaloosa Road~~, thence W with said road to point of beginnin, all in Section 6,
All of said property being located in Township 11, Range 1 East.
Less and Except an undivided one-half interest in and to all mineral and mining rights.

Situated in Blount County, Alabama

MARGINAL:

      The indebtedness hereby secured is satisfied in full
      this 24 day of August, 1966.
                         THE BANK OF BLOUNTSVILLE
                         BY EDNA LEE RUTHERFORD
         Witness: ATTORNEY IN FACT
              JURIETHA PASS
              PROBATE CLERK

Deed shows a separation of Tuscaloosa Road and Huntsville Road behind the Freeman House in Blountsville. Original is the property of Blountsville Historical Society, permission given December 2017.

Frances Darnell Whited

Going for a Ramble

As I am drawing near the closing of my adventure with words, pictures, and old roads, I reflect on my journey. I realized I have become a storyteller like my Grandpa Albert. He would be proud of me. When the great-grandkids came for a visit from Alaska, I decided to try out my skills. Lukus, promoted to first grade, and Alyssa would be a third grader. This age group knows what makes for a good story. I started my story for them with the famous phrase, "Once upon a time." "Once upon a time, there was a young man named Lukas and a young lady named Alyssa. In 2017, they lived in the faraway state called Alaska." So, their story began with a homemade book for their visit to my house on the hill.

We walked again, as we did the year before, around the small spaces of my yard. They remembered my garden and how I broke herbs for them to smell. I told them about the article the local newspaper wrote about my little project for the butterflies. I got the article with the pictures and showed them where the pictures were taken. I planted tiny seeds in the fertile soil of children's minds. I didn't know if they would grow.

They came again to spend the night. I had no idea how to entertain these two very bright children. Before dark, we walked around the garden again. The milkweed was still blooming and seed pods were forming. I talked to them about the beautiful monarchs and other endangered critters. I told them about what I grew and why. We looked at the huge leaves on the native magnolia. I explained to them I wrote stories about our family and how important stories and books were. The sun went down, but there were hours before their bedtime. But, those tiny seeds I planted began to germinate. Alyssa wanted to type her stories on my computer. Lukas and I sat in the recliner with Dennis Martin's book and talked about a story Pawpaw Phillip Whited had told him about "ole red eye." We settled down in the special room where I type.

Alyssa typed three stories that night: *A Dog's Proud Life, Roses,* and *We Were Fishing.* I printed three copies of each story and put them in folders. One was for her. The other two were for her grandparents, Hanh and Bart. Did we have a possible writer or storyteller? Alyssa fell asleep in my chair in front of the computer. I rolled the chair quietly to her waiting bed.

Alyssa and Lukus Harrison

Lukus, my deep thinker, told me he wanted a special room for his projects. While Alyssa typed, we talked about the butterflies, and he used our blanket to become a chrysalis. He showed me how a chrysalis finally becomes a beautiful butterfly. There was much conversation about the truth of the story about "ole red eye," a story told around Blount County and included in Dennis Martin's book. He wanted a copy of *Grandpa's Porch Swing Stories*. I stopped for a few minutes to lock the doors for the night. When I came back, Lukus was a sleeping chrysalis in my old blanket with the book beside him. I picked him up and put him to bed. He slept on.

The children went back to Alaska, and the next day, I went for a "ramble" with a friend from high school. There are many wonderful back roads in Blount County, where you usually only meet the cars of the people who live on them. I finished my story about Uncle Dewey and wanted to find his grave and his sister, Etta Belle's grave.

Our journey took us to find Mt. Tabor Cemetery, and it's not located by Mt. Tabor Church. We rode to Blountsville and took a left toward Garden City. We roamed the amazing back roads of Blount County like our parents did on Saturday and Sunday evenings. We both knew stories about the area. He laughed when I told him about the bottomless spring on the right. If Grandpa Albert told it, it had to be true. There is a water treatment building there now.

We found Mt. Tabor at the end of an old, dusty road, seldom traveled. We questioned why it was miles from the church. That's got to be another story. My friend told me cemeteries are supposed to face the east, for the coming of Christ. I didn't remember that Biblical story. A cool breeze blew, and I heard dryness in the leaves.

Mt. Tabor Cemetery, Blountville, Alabama

We all have stories, children and adults. Our fast, modern world silences our words and old-fashioned storytelling. We all need a quiet "ramble" down an old county road. It frees the words in our head. We hear the echoes of the voices and laughter from long ago as we stroll into the past. We all can be storytellers.

A Spanish Oak Tree and Two Southern Gentlemen

It was another cool morning, May 6, 2018, and the **First Sunday in May.** I'm going to Austin Creek Cemetery as an adult, not as small child. Memories of my little brother filled my thoughts. Just like I did as a child, I put on my Decoration Day clothes and shoes. Thoughts of the past two years of writing crossed my mind. I was full of sentimental feelings. This day was going to be different from all the other trips on the first Sunday in May. I'd still drive the familiar road past Fowler Springs and Mr. Fowler's beautiful white home. I'd think of the huge rock that used to be in the dusty old road going to the church. I would imagine my dad standing under the Hickory tree with the men folks.

Times have changed. The road is paved. Dad and Jerry died. Wilburn Beavers bought the Fowler home, and it's being renovated. Fowler Springs Church has a modern church behind the little white church. And where is Tuscaloosa Road in this story? I am meeting two southern gentlemen who helped me with information about both Austin Creek and Fowler Springs. For about two months, I chased a thin thread of hope for one more deed which named Tuscaloosa Road as a boundary. I promised myself, if this thread does not lead to another deed, I stop looking. I am finished!

With recorder, notebook, pencils, manuscript, and cell phone, I was ready for whatever came my way. It was nine o'clock and my stomach felt a little uneasy. I wanted this day to produce that deed. As I drove in front of the old church, I saw the two southern gentlemen, Wilburn Beavers and Billy Fowler, waiting for me. Together, we talked and walked around the cemetery. They told me about the location of long ago churches on the land, the Austin creek, and old graves. I got enough information to write an article for the new book the museum will publish. They didn't remember why "Austin" was used in the names. The wind was a bit cold so we decided to go into the church. I hadn't been inside since I was a little girl. It was almost overwhelming and the feeling was back in my stomach. We sat on the pews in beautiful little white building before services. I recorded information about both Austin Creek and Fowler Springs. We didn't talk about the folder in Billy's hand. These two fellows have the most wonderful stories! They lived the history in this area. Billy's family donated the land for Fowler Springs Church and also the land for Mt. Tabor Cemetery. Billy saved old family deeds. As I listened, the thought came to me, "Here's another book!"

Billy finished his story, and he opened the folder. There inside were copies of old deeds, his detailed map of the old Tuscaloosa Road, and a picture of the Spanish Oak tree on Tuscaloosa Road. One deed even referenced Joel Johnson! It was a treasure trove, beyond all my hopes. I felt warm tears in my eyes. I am complete. No more searching.

Wilburn drove me down Fowler Springs Road a few days earlier. He showed me pieces of the old roadbed. Today, together, they helped me understand where the old road left the modern Highway 231, below Blountsville. I understood the route it took to Fowler Springs. They both agreed it also ambled down in front of the old Grigsby homeplace at what is now called King's Bend.

Photo taken from yard of Fowler home toward the East. Tree at top is the Spanish Oak tree located on West side of the OLD TUSCALOOSA ROAD
Tree was used as a starting point for Land lines.
Photo taken 1935

The great gift of the photograph taken in 1935 is a gift from Billy Fowler. The old house in the background belonged to Billy's grandparents, David M. and Sarah (Faile) Fowler. The house is longer there. The tree died and nothing is left. The Spanish Oak tree is in the legal description of the property on Tuscaloosa Road.

With as many words of thank you that I could find, I told both Wilburn and Billy what this information meant to me. Only folks who have searched with a bit of hope and a lot of persistence could understand the value of the day.

And just to add to document for the future, **<u>Yes</u>**, there are two springs at Fowler Springs! No more confusion. It really is Fowler Springs. The other spring is behind the old barn, off the road, at the Fowler homeplace.

What else is left to say?

Kind of conveyance...... Warranty Deed
Date of conveyance...... Dec. 10, 1889
Kind of acknowledgment...... proper
Separate acknowledgment by wife...... yes
Date of acknowledgment...... Dec. 10, 1889
Are all grantors named in acknowledgment?...... yes
Are parties signing named in body of deed?...... yes
Before whom } James R. Wooten, J.P.
Acknowledged } Blount County, Ala.,
Date of filing for record...... Dec. 8, 1892
Recorded in Book...... Z ...... Page...... 565
Is is properly indexed?...... yes
Is dower properly conveyed?...... yes
Is homestead properly conveyed by wife?...... yes
Consideration $ 5.00
Is it recited in deed as paid?...... yes

Jacob Pullan and wife
Mary Ann Pullan.
Grantor.

To

Joseph Holley

Grantee.

Part of the DESCRIPTION OF PROPERTY CONVEYED SEC. 36 TP. 11-1-West
South-east fourth of North-east quarter of
Commencing at a spanish oak tree on the west of the
Tuscaloosa road; thence north running with said road
120 yards to the corner of old apple orchard; on the
east of said road; thence East to the Meridian;
thence South to Joseph Holley corner; on the Meridian;
thence west to the commencing point, containing two
acres, more or less, in Blount County, Ala.;

Documents Tuscaloosa Road and the Spanish oak tree, near present day Fowler Springs Church, Blountsville, Alabama. Original is property of Billy Fowler.

Old Dogs and an End to a Dusty Road

When I awoke this morning, I looked at the three boxes of family pictures as I walked to the kitchen for my morning cup of coffee. I thought of those migrating Rose Breasted Grosbeaks who fought over seeds for their breakfast. They left for their home up north. A feeling of sadness for things gone came over me. I sat on my porch, enjoying the taste and smell of coffee. It has been good to meet and honor these people from the past. I asked myself, "When should I stop writing about them?" There are still so many wonderful pictures and lots of dusty roads.

Darnell Playin' in the Dirt on the Old Tuscaloosa Road

If I listen carefully, echoes of voices from the Old Tuscaloosa Road come back. I envision Uncle T.C., tall and thin as a hoe handle, swinging my mom around and around. It delights me to know I drank sweet well water from those common family dippers. There was pleasure in the fact I learned to drive a straight shift car down the same dusty road my dad drove as a young man going to Austin Creek. I sipped water from Fowler Spring like my Grandma Grigsby. I stood at the grave of Joel Johnson in Guinn's Grove. I placed flowers on the grave of Oliver Johnson, who died in the flu pandemic. I marvel at the bold and hardy pioneers of my family who came to Blount County, Alabama. Oh my, I have lived a full life with great memories and a family full of characters. I heard a former Blount County boy say on television, "Some people think back roads means backwards." Our Southern dialect, love of nature, and old traditions confuse some modern city people. The old, dusty back roads of Blount County formed our character and spirit. As the dust rose around us, the roads were with us as we learned about honesty. They were there as we learned about respect and love.

It was not always an easy journey. A wide range of emotions would sometimes overwhelm me as I wrote. But, for this period in time, I did what I started out to do, give a voice to the Old Tuscaloosa Road and some other dusty roads of Blount County. Sipping my coffee, I sat and thought: Somewhere, there are still pieces of the old roadbed waiting for one more story. Like the mountains on all sides of me, the stories surround me and wait to be put on paper. Barefooted children race down a hill, old men in large black hats sit in straight back chairs and tell tall tales. Highfalutin' city folk come for fresh vegetables grown on Grandpa Albert's farm. It was on a dusty road I developed my independent spirit and gained a better understanding of those "characters" from my past. I smiled at my sentimental thoughts. After all these years, I'm still just a Blount County girl from old Tuscaloosa Road.

Molly, Waiting for her Human

Miss Molly waited patiently for our morning walk. I found my walking shoes and hiking canes my son brought me, and we headed out to see the morning. I know we are in the winter of our days. Our path up the hill is beginning to cover in fall leaves. The trail is dusty from the dry summer with little dirt clouds rising from our steps. I smelled dust. I paused for a moment, bent down like I did as the curly haired girl from Tuscaloosa Road. I used my shoe to loosen the ground and picked up a hand full of dirt. I let it slowly slip though my fingers. The wind carried it away.

There's an old Native American quote from a book I read often, ***Indian Spirit,*** that says it all. "The ground on which we stand is sacred ground. It is the dust and blood of our ancestors." My mind filled with memories of other walks, echoing voices from my past, old friends and old dogs who have gone on and finished with the journey of life. A dove cooed far away. It didn't hear us coming. I heard the pine trees whisper softly, felt the kiss of the morning sun, and once again wondered where all those kin folks have gone.

As my journey of life slows down, I realize I am more than the DNA of my ancestors. As I traveled across the mountains, through the valleys, and down the dusty roads of Blount County, Alabama, I collected memories and stories. I watched and listened to the people who lived here. I developed relationships, some were good, and some were not so good. A better understanding of Blount County and this native girl evolved. Ending, I smile and quote from a book by the Alabama author and educator Harvey Jackson. He summed up my feelings accurately as I close, "And in considering our journey, where we began, where we are now, and where we are going, we can find comfort in a prayer one preacher, maybe an Alabama preacher, once prayed:

>Dear God:
>We ain't what we ought to be.
>We ain't what we gonna be.
>We ain't what we wanta be.
>But, thank God,
>We ain't what we was."

Frances Darnell Whited

Epilogue

During my twenty-five year career in education, I read hundreds of books for children. My favorite time spent sitting in my rocking chair in the Elementary Media Center at Oneonta City School, reading delightful children's literature. I was the queen of drama on my personal stage, the library. It's easy to tell if you had a good story by looking in those young eyes. During those days, I didn't read a lot of books for grown folks or any Blount County literature. Working my way toward a book about my family, I found a new love in the stories of Blount County, Alabama, and Native American literature. Listed below are those books which kept me focused on my journey. They have a special place in my home and my life, and they helped me give a voice to my dusty old roads and their people. They made it possible for me to find the spirit to write, gave me smiles, a few tears, a love of words, and they will never be forgotten.

1. *Sketches of Alabama*, Mary Gordon Duffee, University of Alabama Press, 1970
2. *Bangor Days Gone By*, Ryan M Cole, 2016
3. *Blount Springs, Alabama's Fountain of Youth*, Greg Burden, 2014
4. *Cleveland, Alabama 35049*, Eldridge Bynum, 1989
5. *The Way It Was Back Then*, Robert Earl Woodard, 2014
6. *Our Patriots of America, World War No. II*, National Patriotic Publishers

7. *The Heritage of Blount County, Alabama, Vol. 5*, 1999
8. *Blount County, Alabama, WWI, Draft Card Abstracts*, Robin Sterling, 2013
9. *People and Things from the Blount County, Alabama News and News-Dispatch 1879-1889*, Robin Sterling, 2006
10. *Tales of Old Blount County, Alabama*, Robin Sterling, 2013
11. *Great Temple of Travel, A Pictorial History of Birmingham Terminal Station 1909-1969*, Marvin Clemons, 2016
12. *Send the Alabamians, World War I Fighters in the Rainbow Division*, Nimrod Frazer, 2014
13. *Grandpa's Porch Swing Stories, Tall Tales of Southern Humor and Folklore*, Dennis Martin, 2014
14. *Murder in Blount County*, Judi McGuire, 2017 (Fiction, but has lots of local color)
15. *Indian Spirit*, edited by Michael Oren Fitzgerald and Judith Fitzgerald, 2006
16. *Miscellaneous Confederate Soldiers from in and around Blount County*, compiled Robin Sterling
17. *The Tragedy and the Triumph of Phenix City, Alabama*, Margaret Anne Barnes, 1998

Frances Darnell Whited

Appendix

My searches for evidence of the existence of the Old Tuscaloosa Road were both tedious and frustrating. I found almost nothing with the name of the old road which ran past my childhood home. Two of the finds were the result of happenstance, rather than any planned search on my part. I have since learned this is a frequent occurrence in searching for missing family connections and old roads.

To complete the record, some of the documents are included substantiate the Old Tuscaloosa Road, or Old Tuscaloosa Pike, as it was also known as, really existed apart from the old Huntsville Road and Huntsville-Tuscaloosa Road.

There is no story for the photograph of the old car and the dusty road. The name on the back is believed to be Willie Wright. Who is Willie Wright? No one in the family remembers him. I imagine driving this amazing car down the rutted Tuscaloosa Road!

Permission to use the Freeman House picture was given by Betty Alexander, Blountsville Historical Society, April 16, 2018.

Freeman House

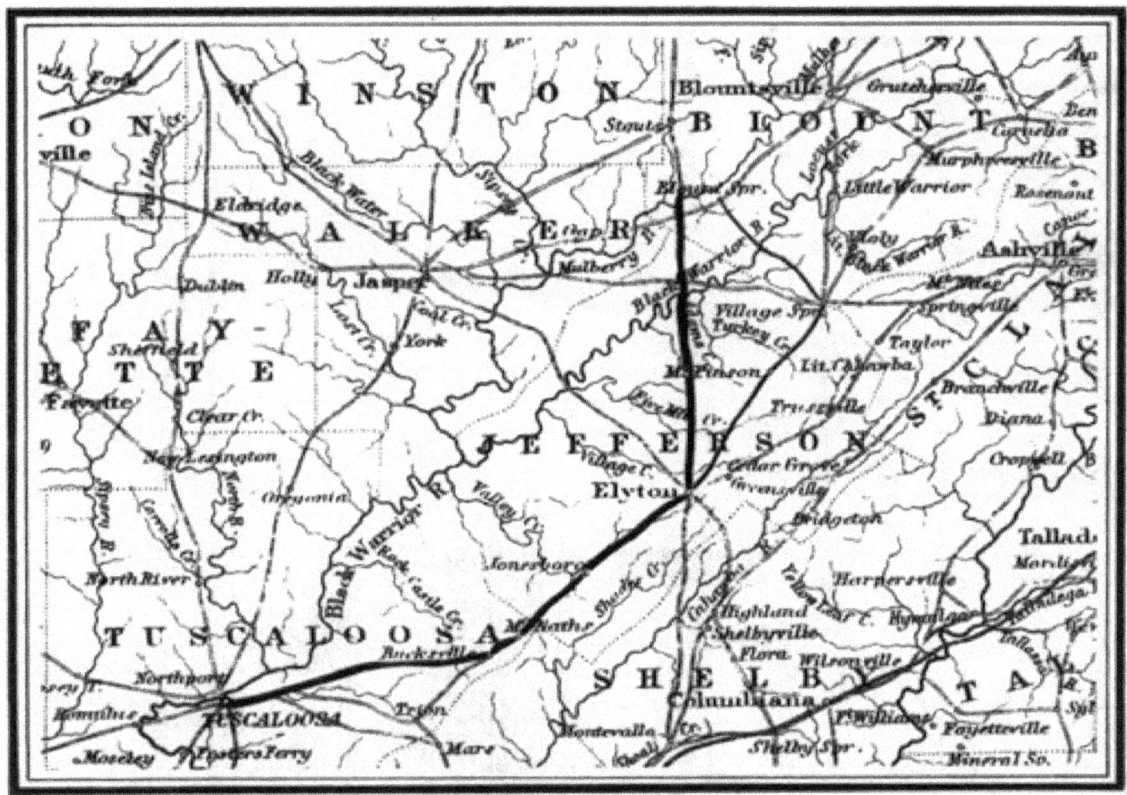

The Old Stage Road on which Mary Gordon Duffee traveled from Tuscaloosa through Elyton, a crossroads of travel, to Blount Springs. (Map section taken from Bartholomew's Alabama map of 1856).

The map above is from Mary Gordon Duffee's book, Sketches of Alabama.

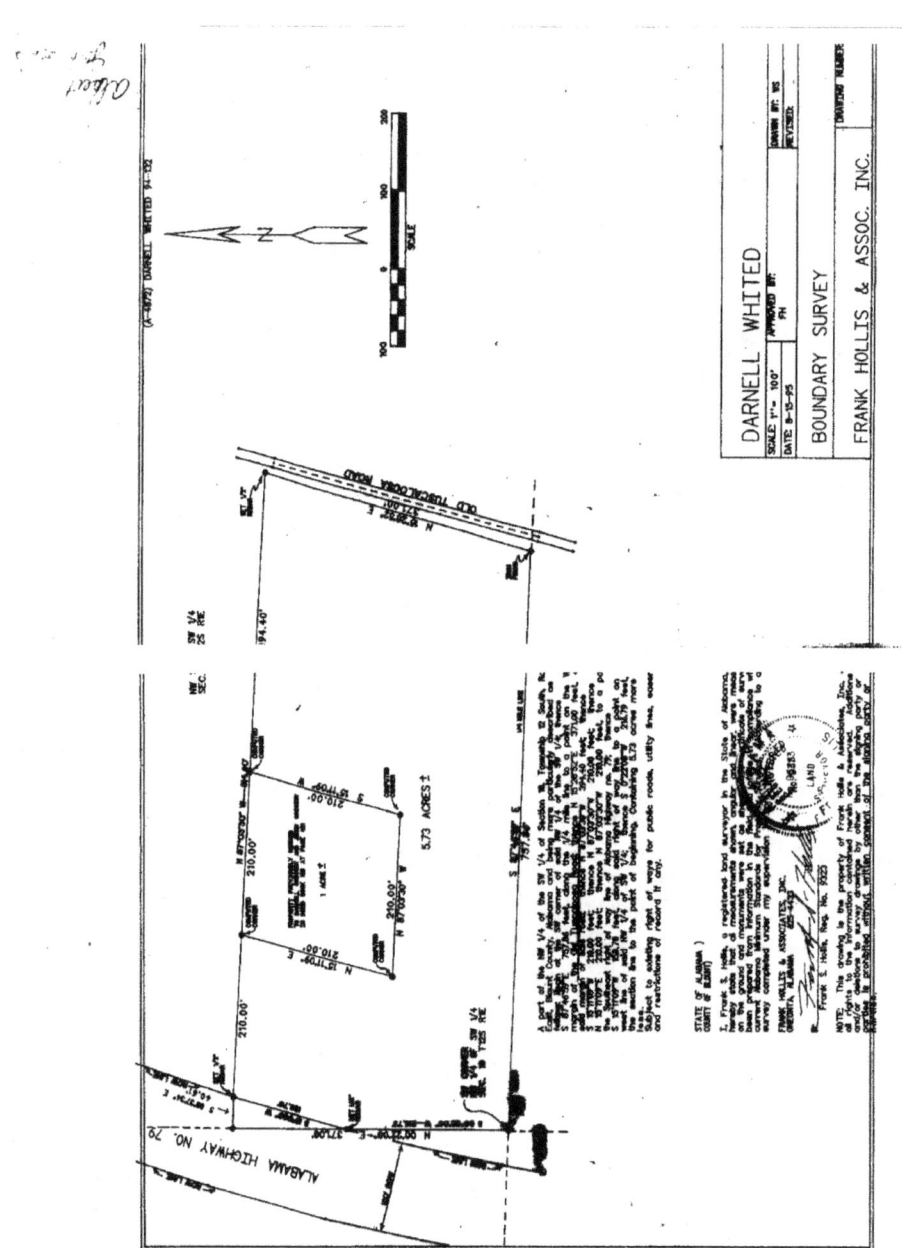

Albert Johnson Property on the Old Tuscaloosa Road

GENERAL WARRANTY DEED

STATE OF ALABAMA
COUNTY OF BLOUNT

KNOW ALL MEN BY THESE PRESENTS: that whereas the historic site commonly known as the "Freeman Cabin" or "Freeman House", together with the acreage on which it stands (hereinafter referred to as the "historic site") situated near Blountsville in Blount County, Alabama, is a landmark along the old Huntsville-Tuscaloosa stagecoach road and is a reminder of Blount County's early days and pioneer heritage; and

Whereas, it is the desire of the current owners of the property, Alma Lee Wright and N. Edward Scott, as well as many area residents (and more particularly the Blountsville and Blount County historical societies) that the said historic site be preserved as part of Blount County's heritage and as a place to educate present and future generations of Blount Countians and Alabamians about their heritage;

The Deed Gifting the Freeman House

Kind of conveyance	Patent
Date of conveyance	Dec. 3, 1831
Kind of acknowledgment	
Separate acknowledgment by wife	
Date of acknowledgment	
Are all grantors named in acknowledgment	
Are parties signing named in body of deed	
Before whom	Certificate No. 4626
Acknowledged	
Date of filing for record	
Recorded in Book	1 Page 180
Is it properly indexed?	yes
Is dower properly conveyed?	
Is homestead properly conveyed by wife?	
Consideration $	
Is it recited in deed as paid?	

United States of America

Grantor.

TO

Joel Johnson,

Grantee

DESCRIPTION OF PROPERTY CONVEYED — SEC. TP. R.
The South-east fourth of North-east quarter of 36 11-1-West, in Blount County, Ala.,

Joel Johnson's property, located on what would become Tuscaloosa Road near Fowler's Springs Church. Original is property of Billy Fowler.

Walking Down Tuscaloosa Road

I remember, when I was young, walking down that old, unpaved country road.
Folks here were mostly farmers; some raised cattle, and others grew row crops.
They tilled the fields, had orchards and planted those large gardens that we hoed.
I'm much older now, perhaps a bit wiser, but I still remember falling raindrops
On the dry, powdery dust on that old road, which was the old Tuscaloosa Road.

It wasn't much of a road back then - unpaved, tree-shaded, packed hard with chert
Taken from the tailings of an old coal mine down the road and beyond the river.
I guess it really doesn't matter that the old road was mostly red, rocky clay dirt.
It held us together, as we lived, laughed and loved, thinking we would live forever
I still recall those good times when we all walked down the old Tuscaloosa Road.

I remember the mud squishing between my toes, when the rain fell on the road;
Being passed by wagons filled with goods, ears of corn, cotton, and bales of hay,
Going to or returning from a nearby town where the loads were bought and sold.
Wondering where they went, and if I could go there some day, wherever that lay.
Such were the times we shared strolling together down the old Tuscaloosa Road.

Those times are gone, and so are the people who lived on that country highway.
Those were times when children listened as the elders spoke of those long gone.
Where did they go, the ones who lived and loved on the road? Where are they today?
What did they do, and did they do well? Who did they marry, or did they die alone?
Do they remember those times when we all walked down the old Tuscaloosa Road?

I remember now as I did then and as I grow older, I realize with a sense of wonder
And of regret, that I did not take the time to stay in touch those friends and kin,
To take time to ask of my elders questions whose answers I now can only ponder.
Of the choices I made, opportunities taken -and lost - where I failed. Once again,
I miss my childhood days, when we went aimlessly down the Old Tuscaloosa Road.

Leonard Yarbrough 2017

Permission to use was given by Leonard Yarbrough.

About the Author

Frances Darnell Grigsby Whited grew up on the Old Tuscaloosa Road in the small town of Cleveland, Alabama. A native-born Blount Countian, she earned her early education from Cleveland School, grammar and high school. She has a B. S. Degree in Elementary Education and a Master's Degree in Educational Media Leadership from the University of Alabama in Birmingham. She obtained a post-Master's Certification in Educational Leadership from the University of Alabama in Tuscaloosa. During her twenty-five year career in education, she worked for the Oneonta City School System serving as an Elementary Media Specialist, Elementary Assistant Principal, and Elementary Principal. Her professional affiliations included the American Library Association, Alabama Library Association, Alabama Instructional Media Association, Guild of Professional Writers for Children, and the Alabama Writers Conclave.

Mrs. Whited currently lives near the Straight Mountain community in rural Blount County. Her family includes one son, Bart Alston Rainey, and his wife, Hanh, two grandchildren and two great-grandchildren. A Master Gardener, she oversees her Monarch Project for the endangered monarch butterfly. Other hobbies include membership in the Blount County Historical Society, genealogy, volunteering and traveling in Belize, hiking with her dogs, driving the old roads of Blount County, and listening to and telling stories about Blount County and its way of life.

She invites you on her journey down the dusty roads of Blount County, Alabama. Who knows? There may be more to come!

Footprints in the Dust

Frances Darnell Whited